SHADOWBOXES

VOLUME 2

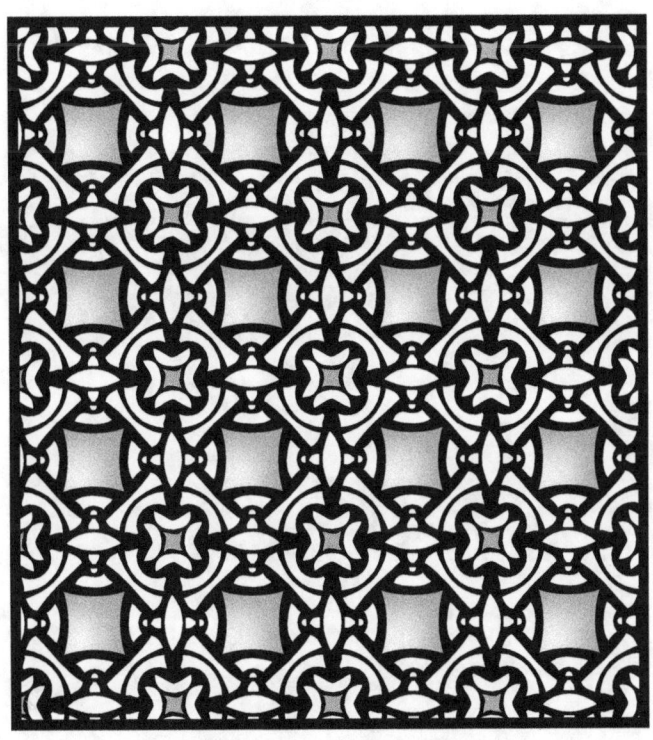

This book is printed on just one side of the paper
to avoid bleed through. If using markers it may be helpful
to place a piece of paper or cardstock behind the page.

To view samples of these illustrations colored by the author please visit
www.lovelyleisure.me

LOVELY LEISURE

ILLUSTRATIONS BY PAULA PARRISH

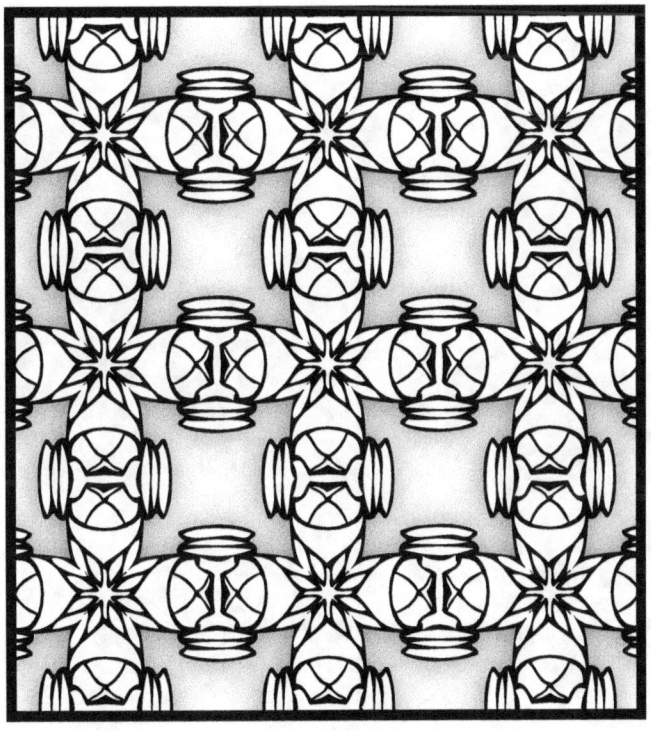

Shadowboxes Volume 2 Coloring Book
© 2016 Paula Parrish

www.lovelyleisure.me

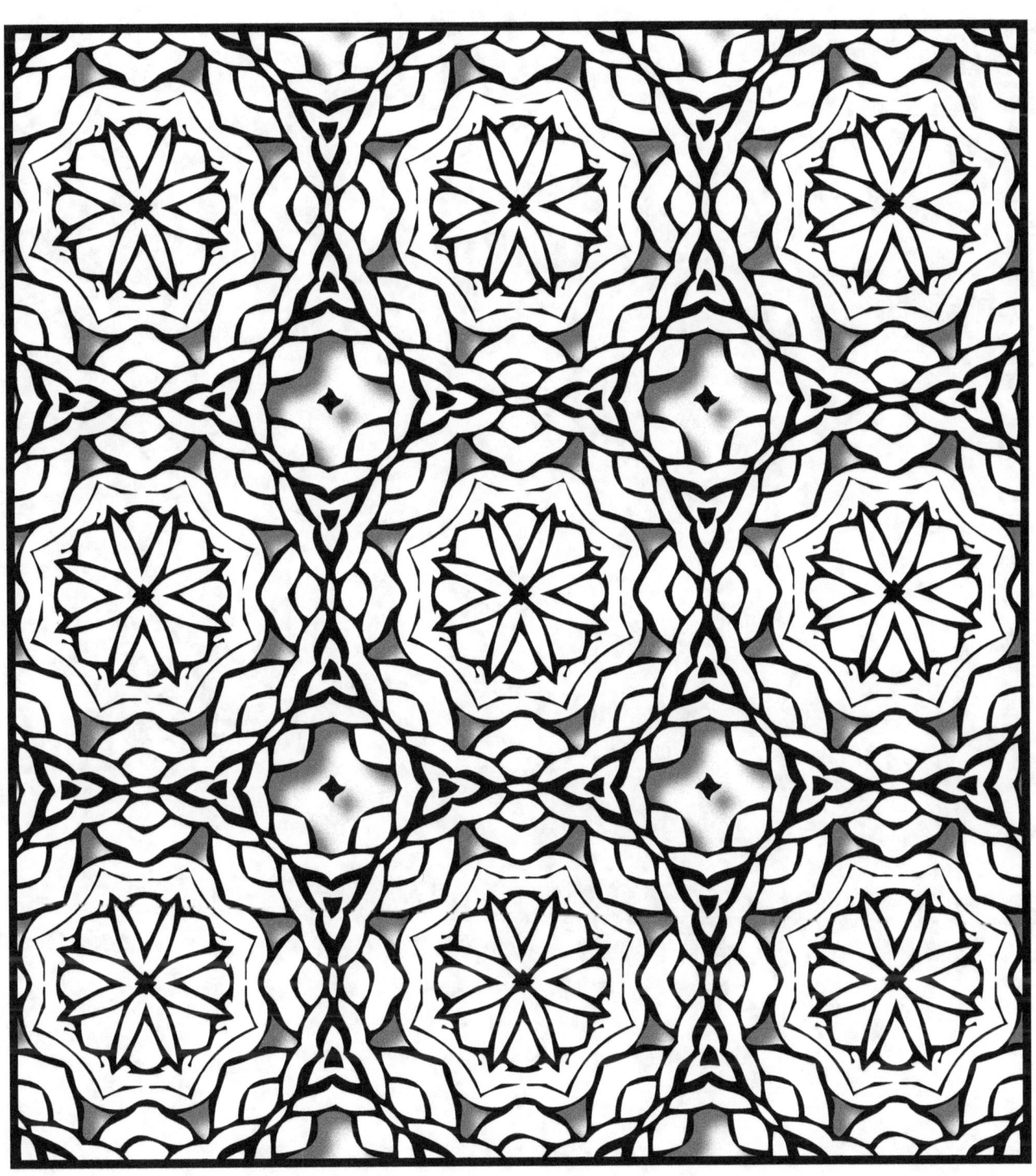

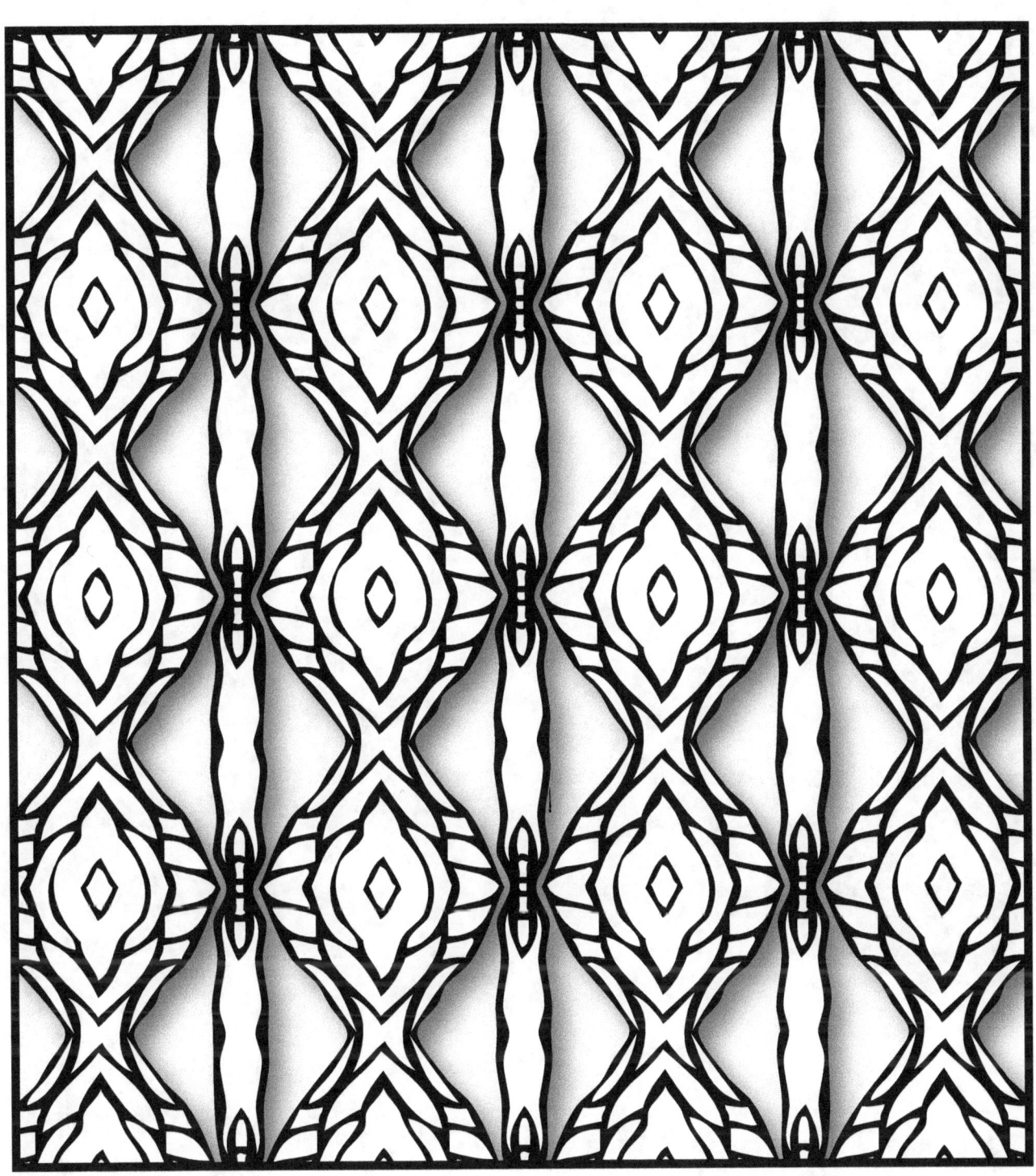

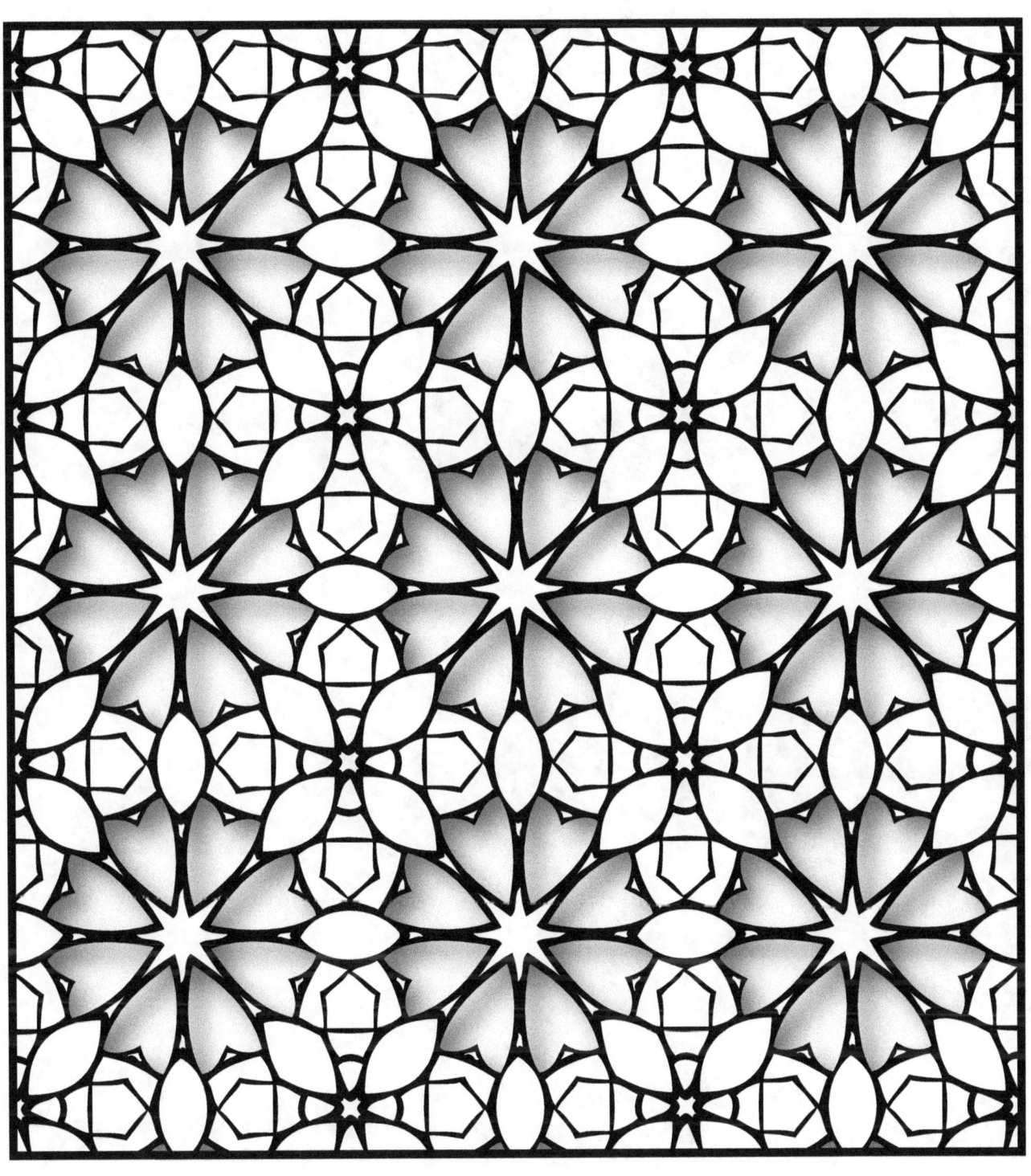

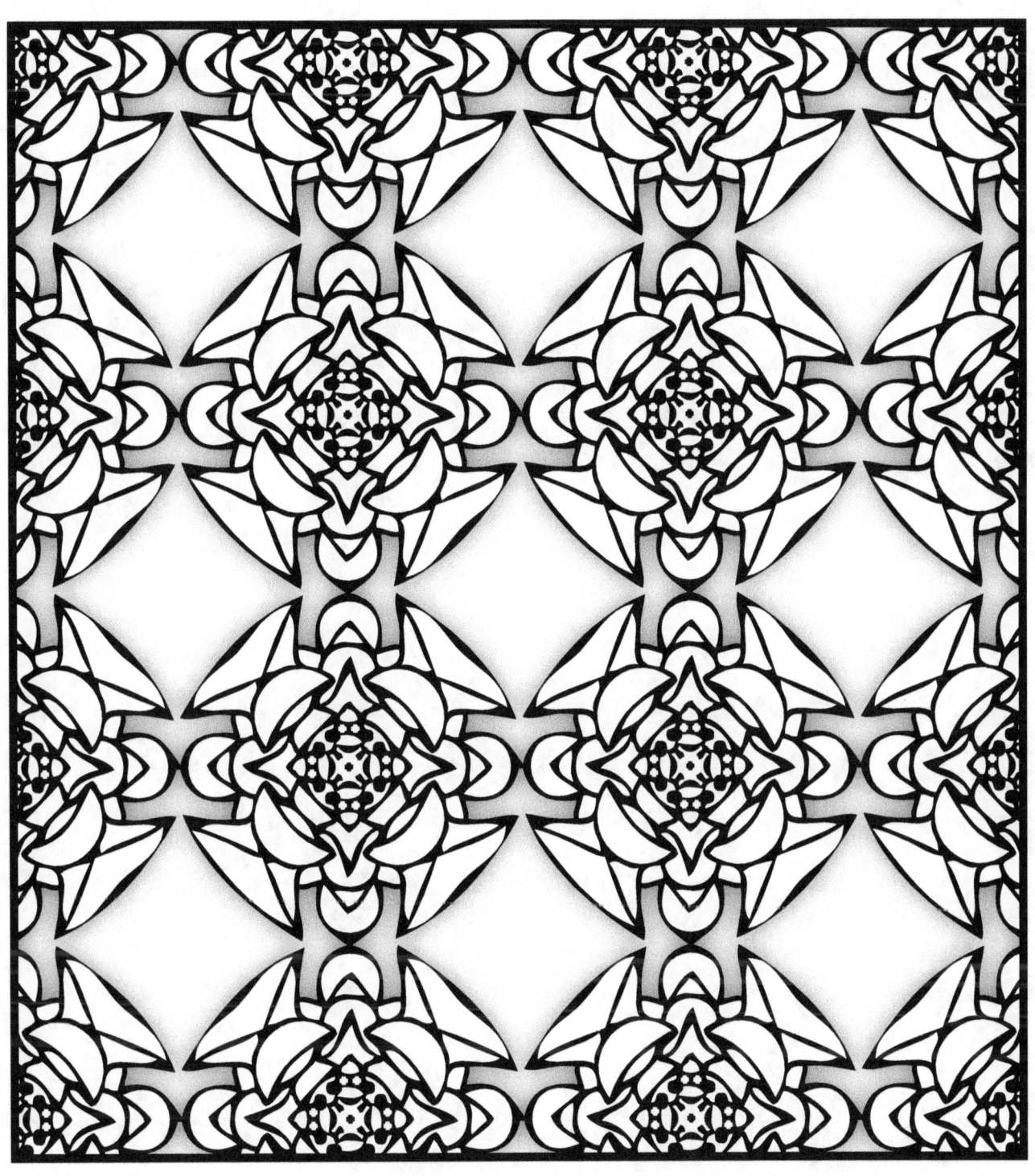

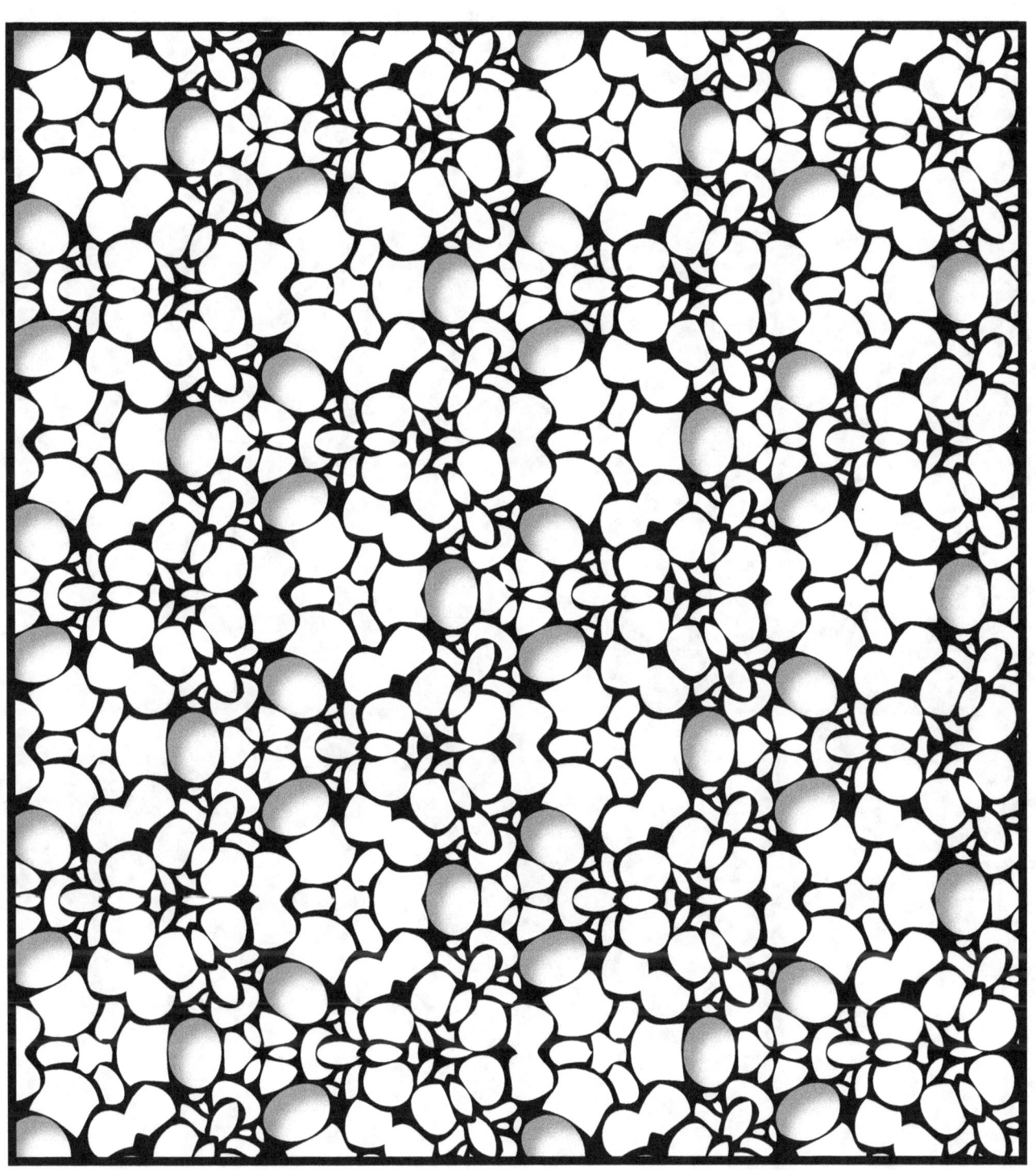

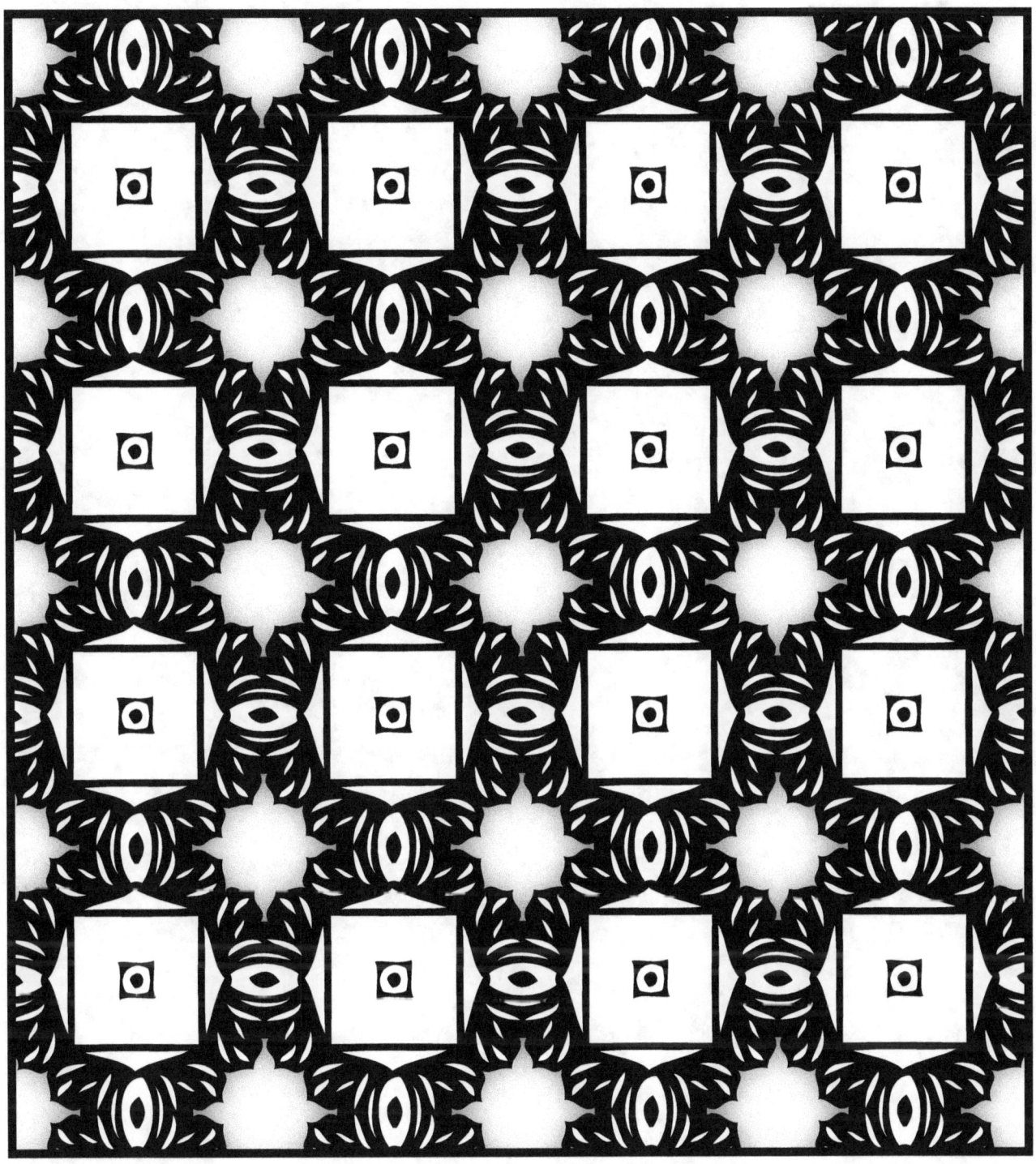

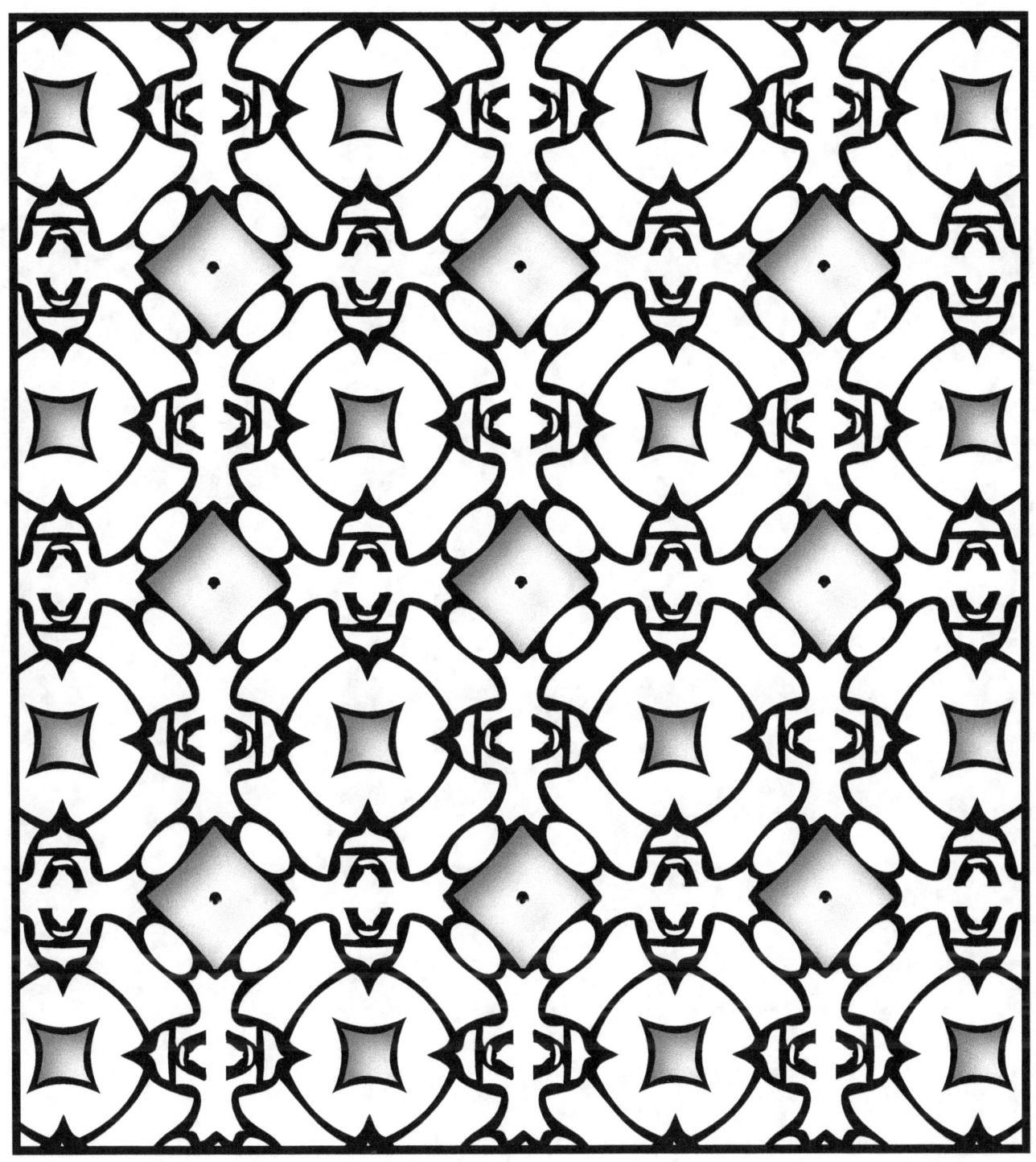

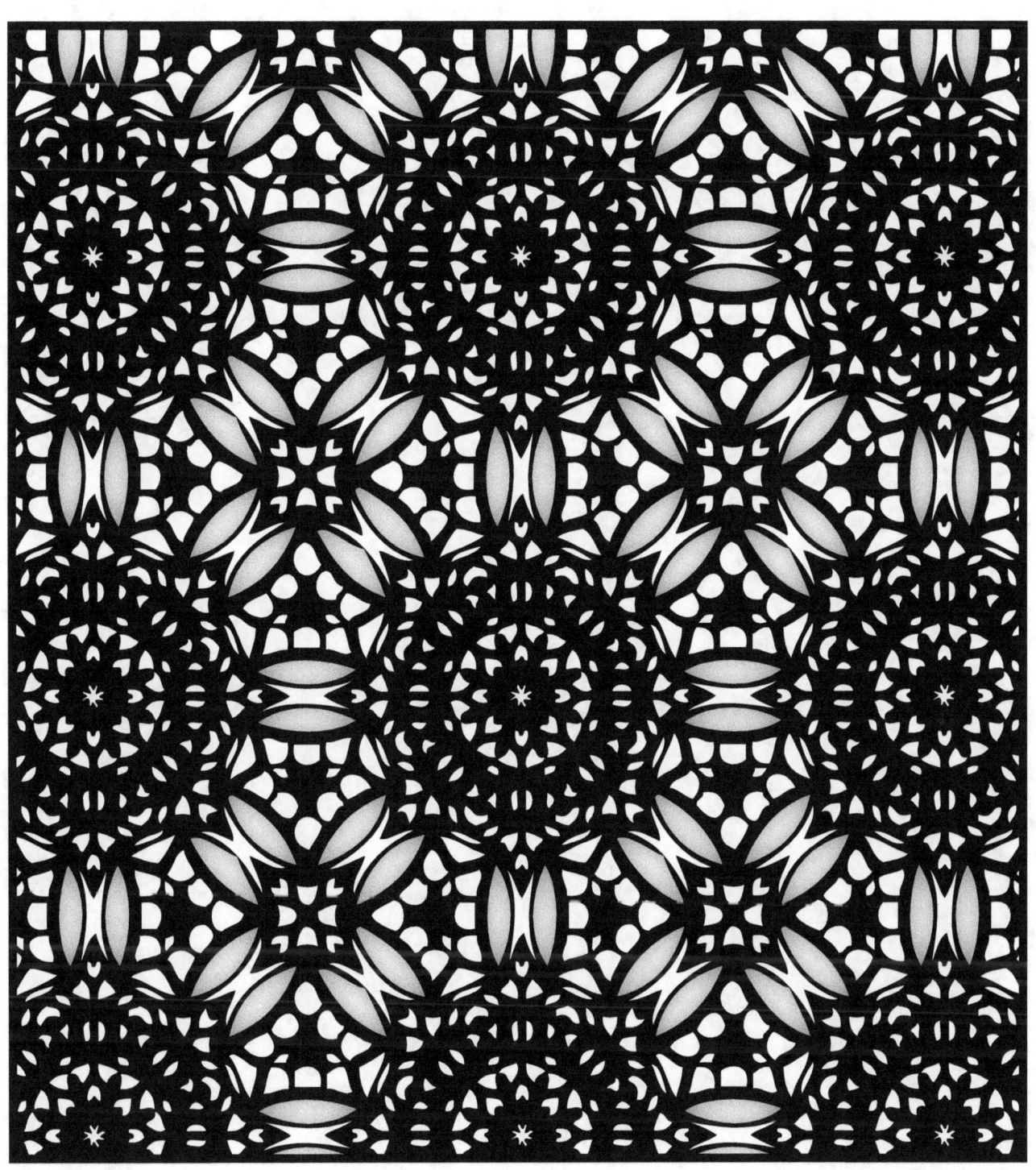

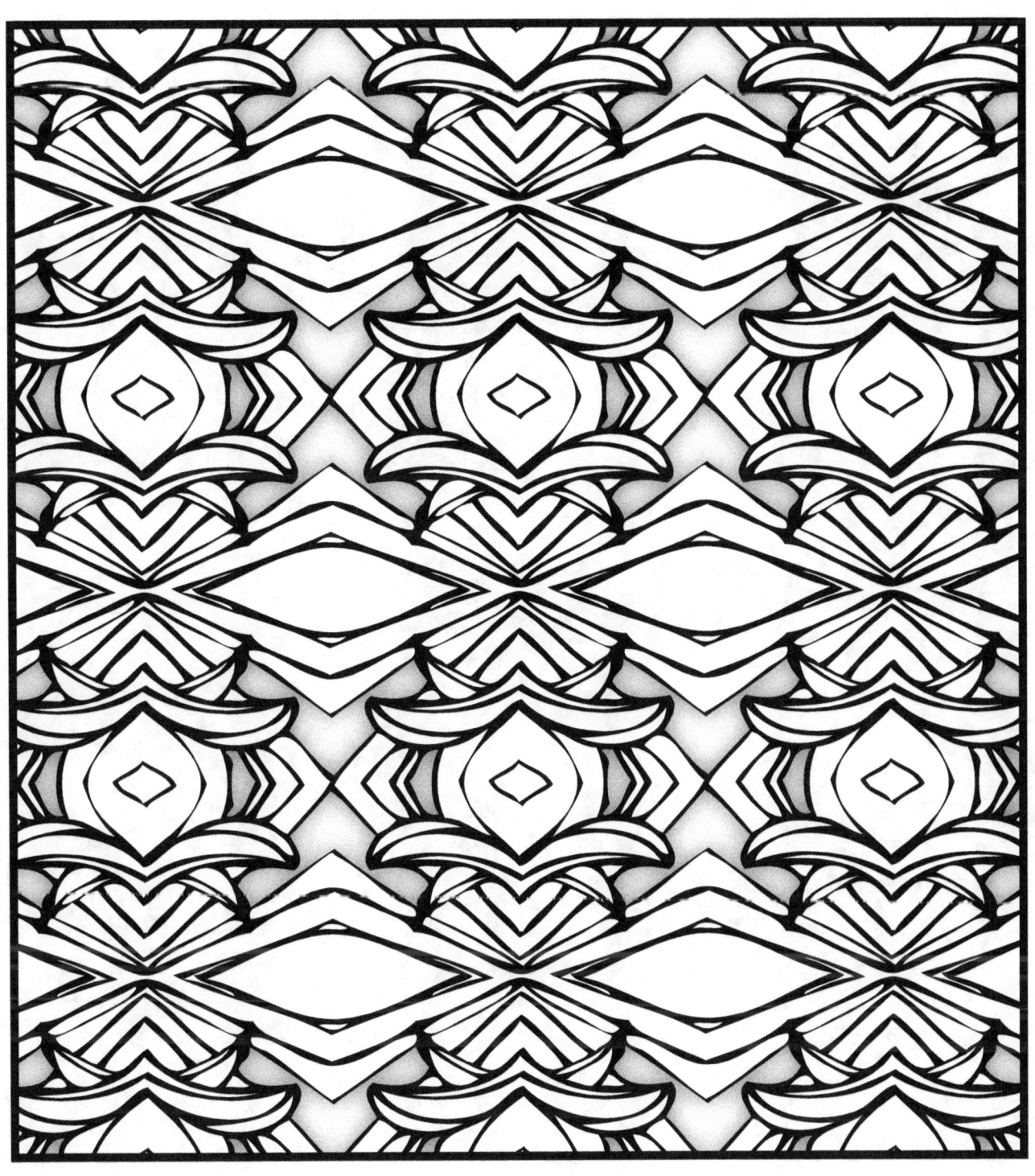

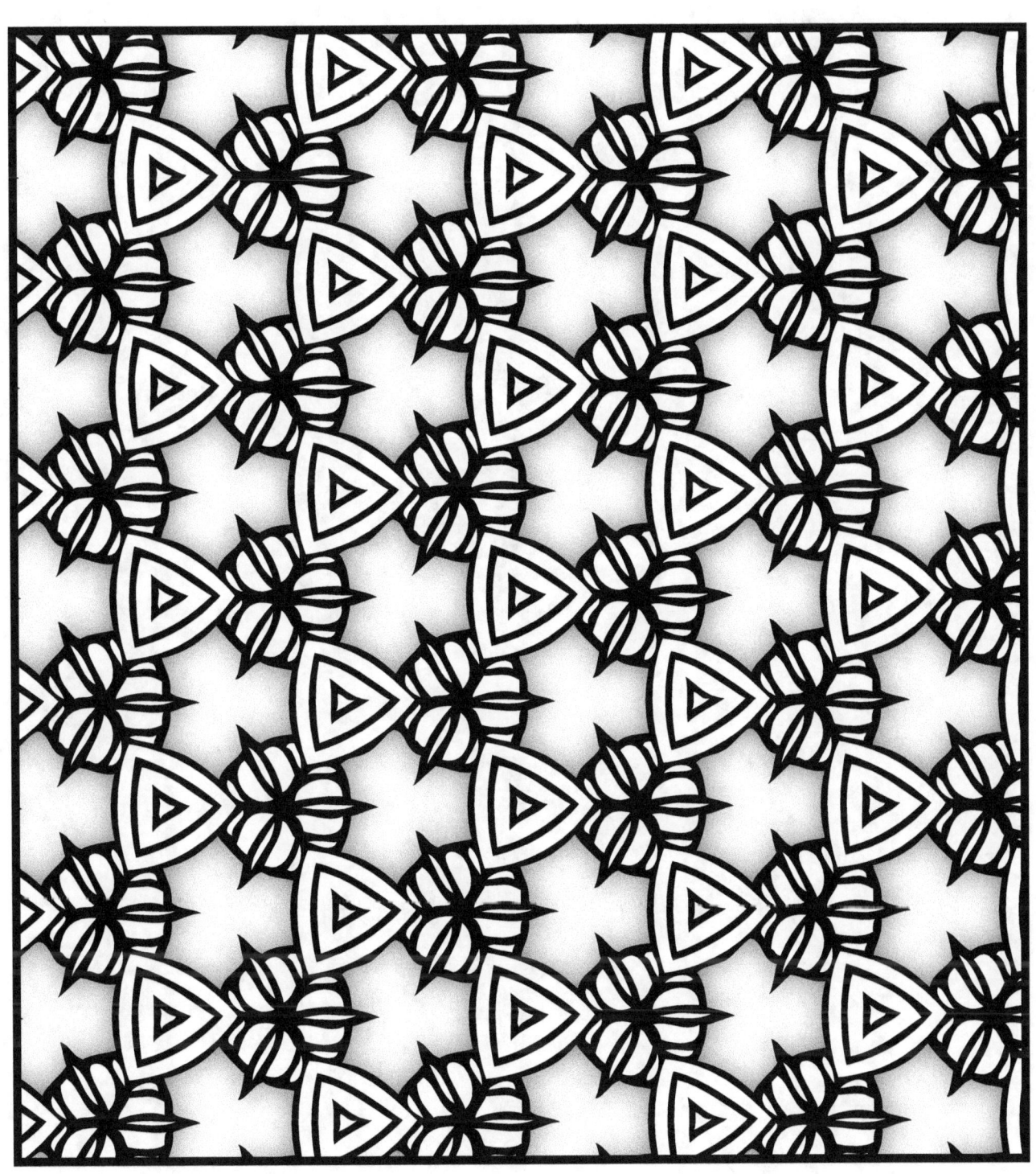

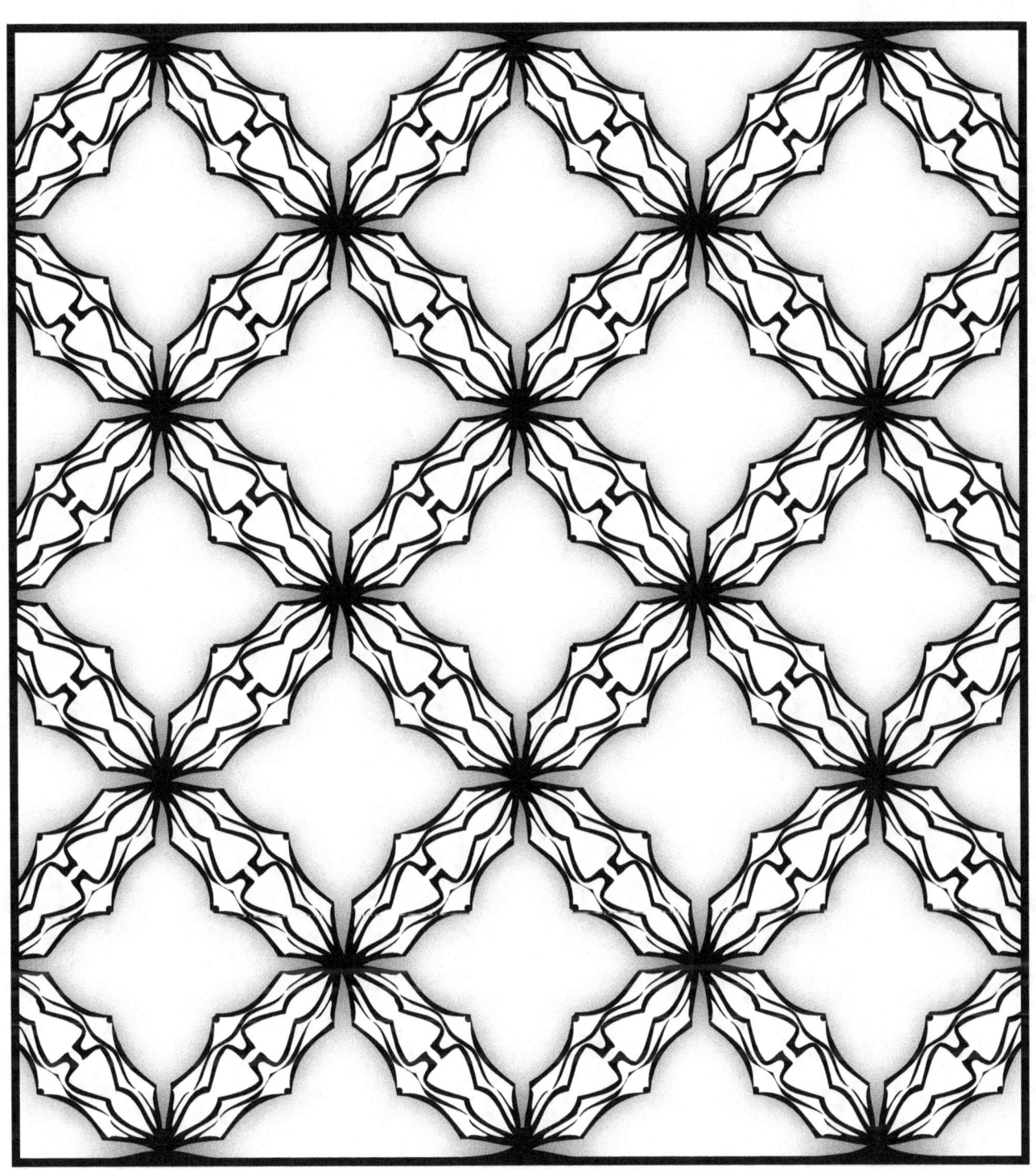

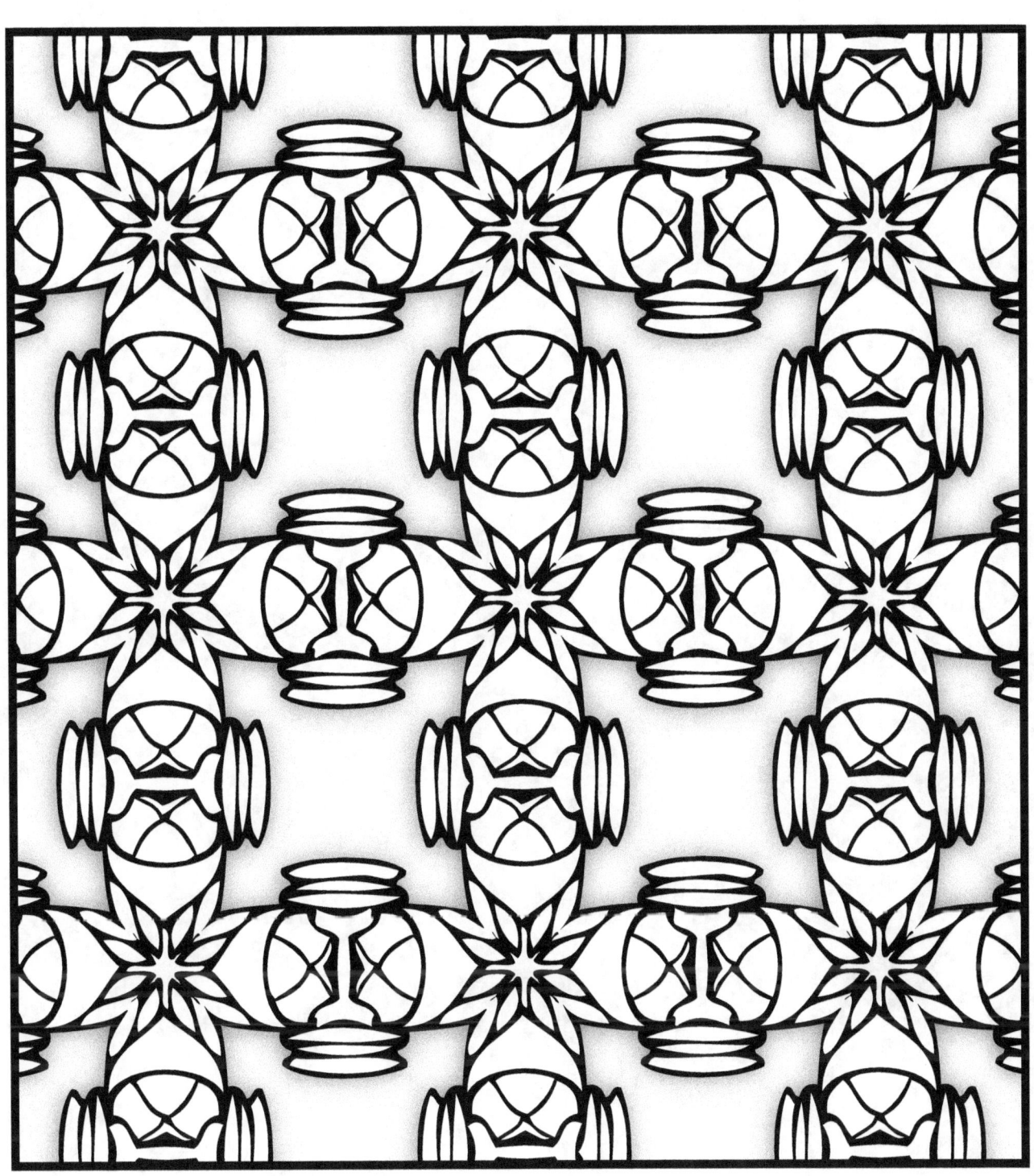

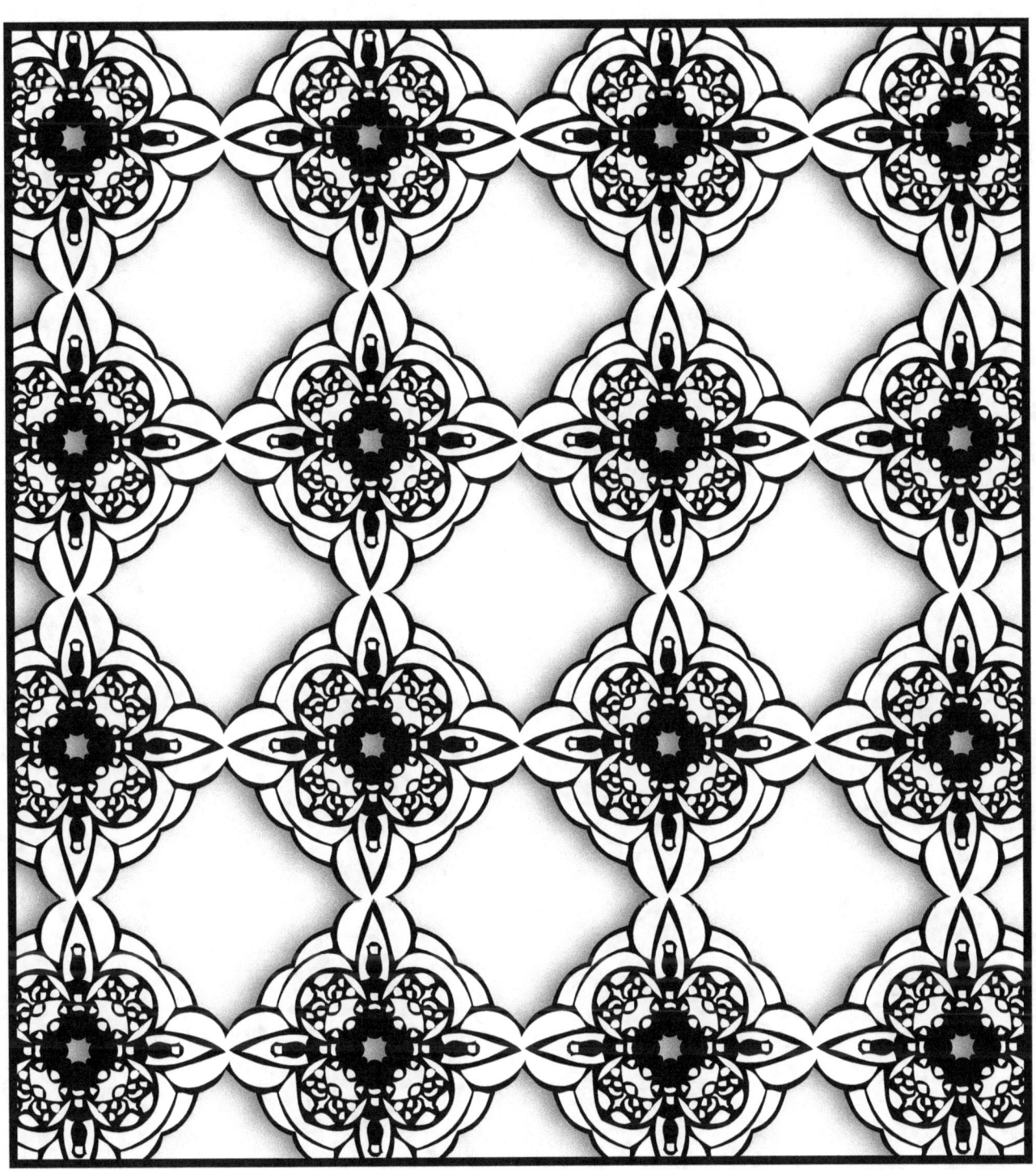

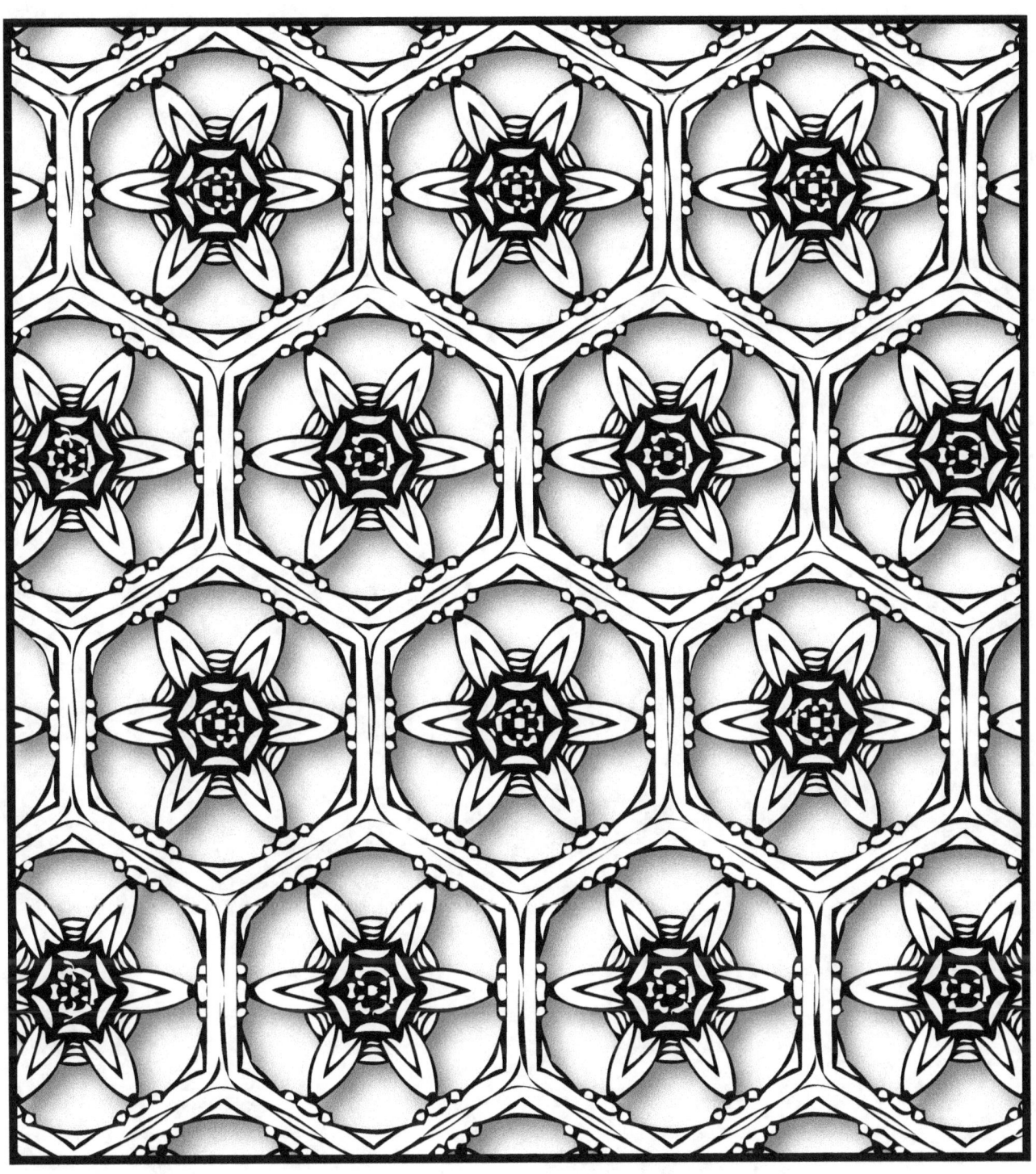

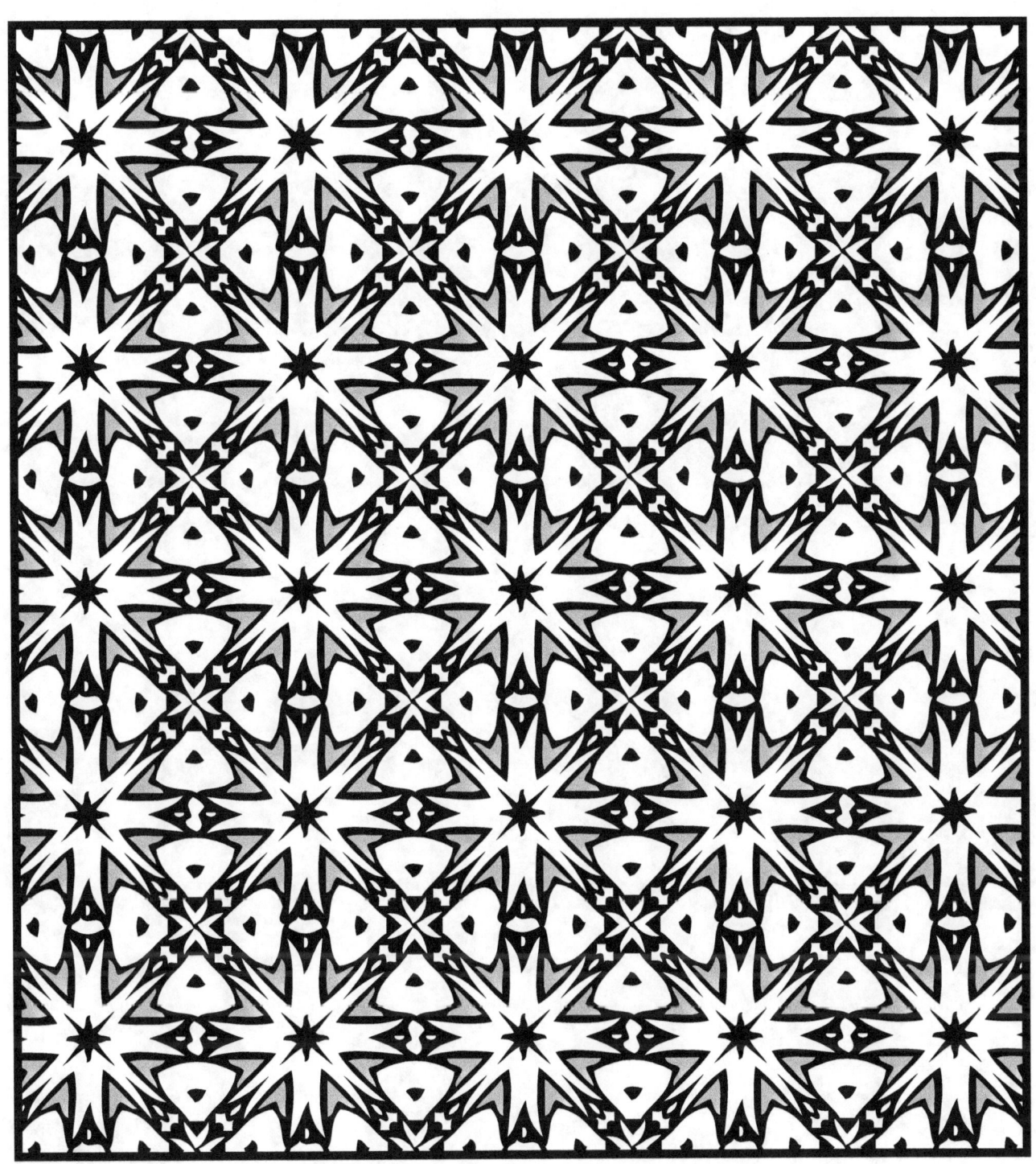

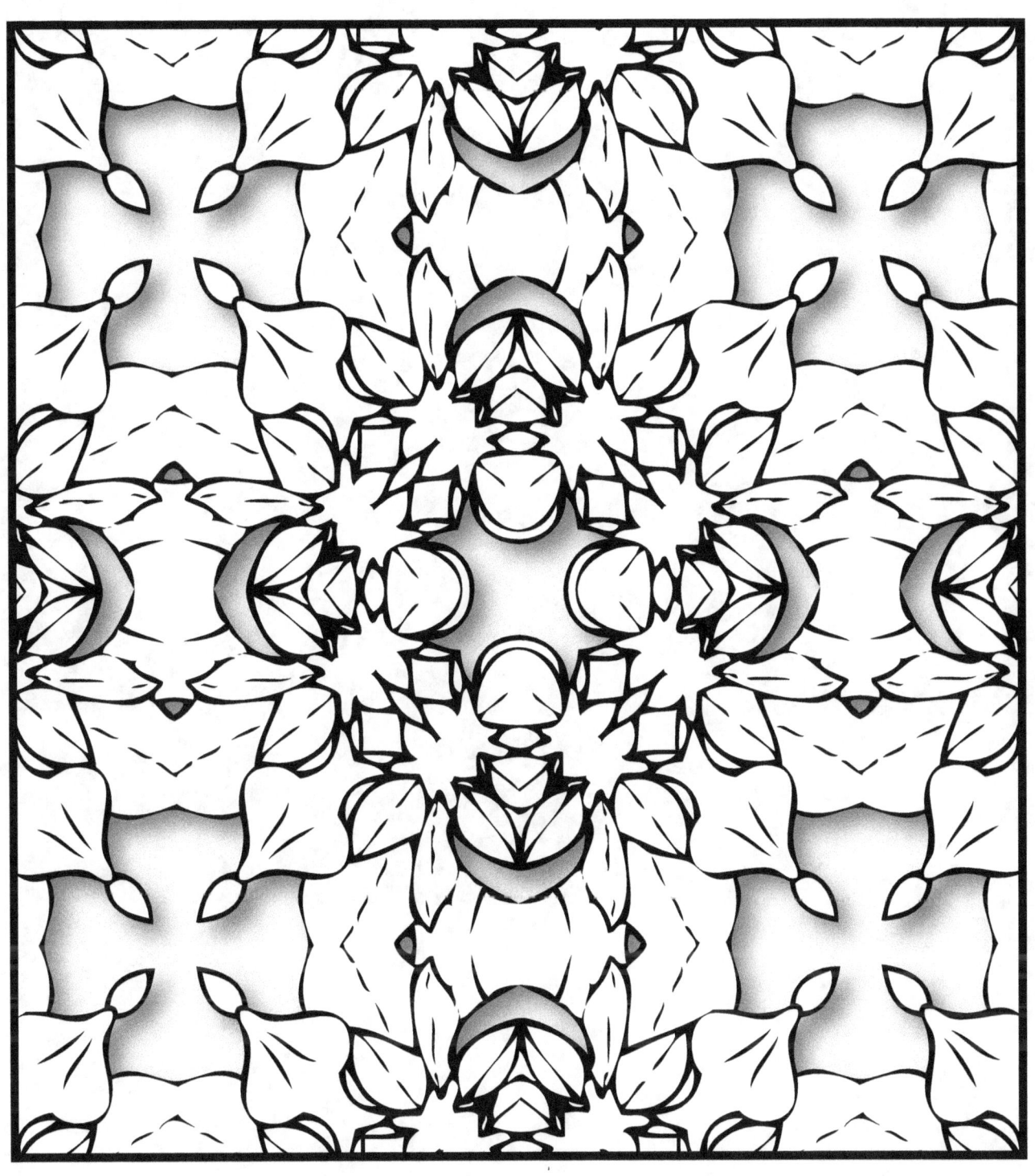

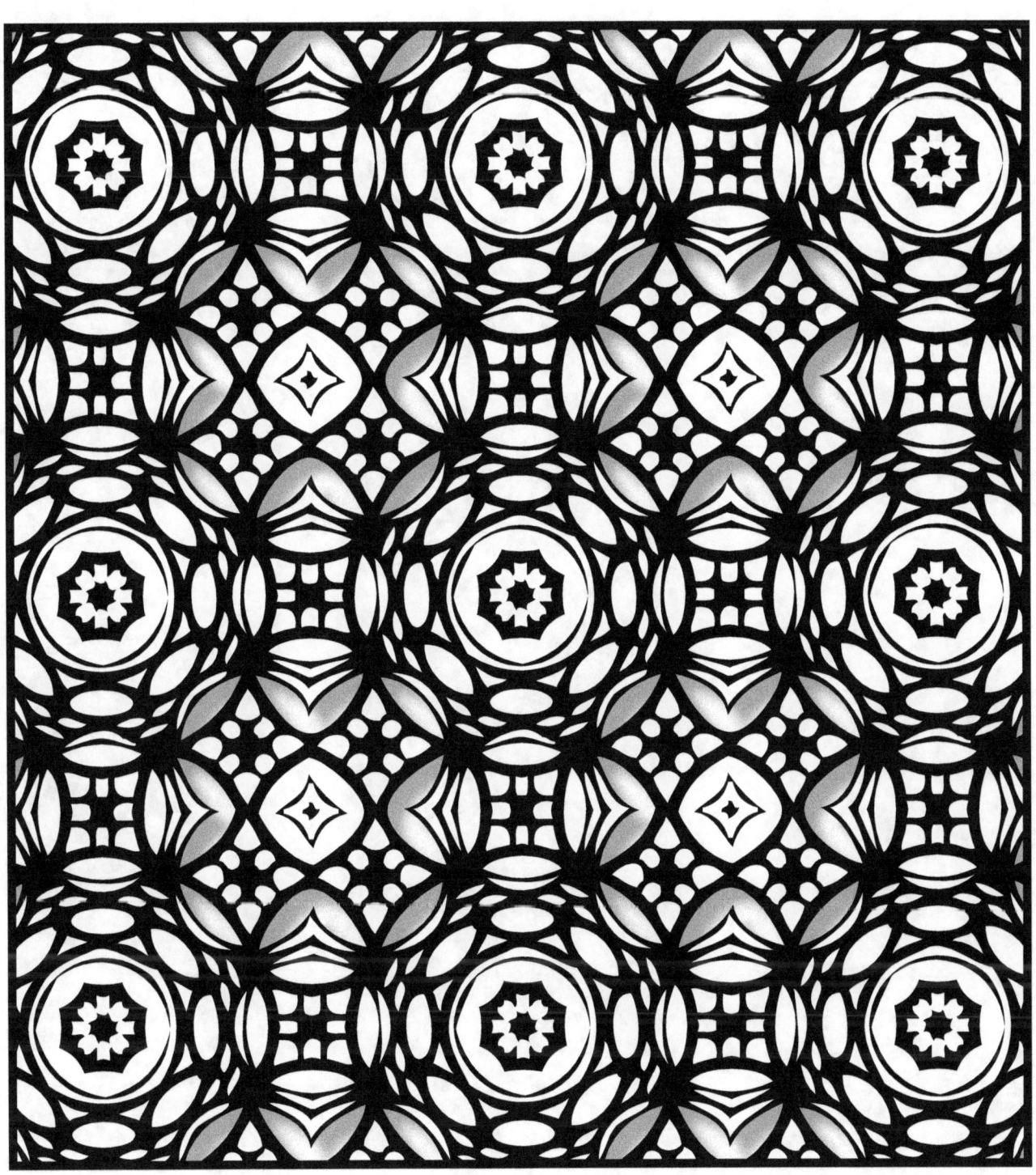

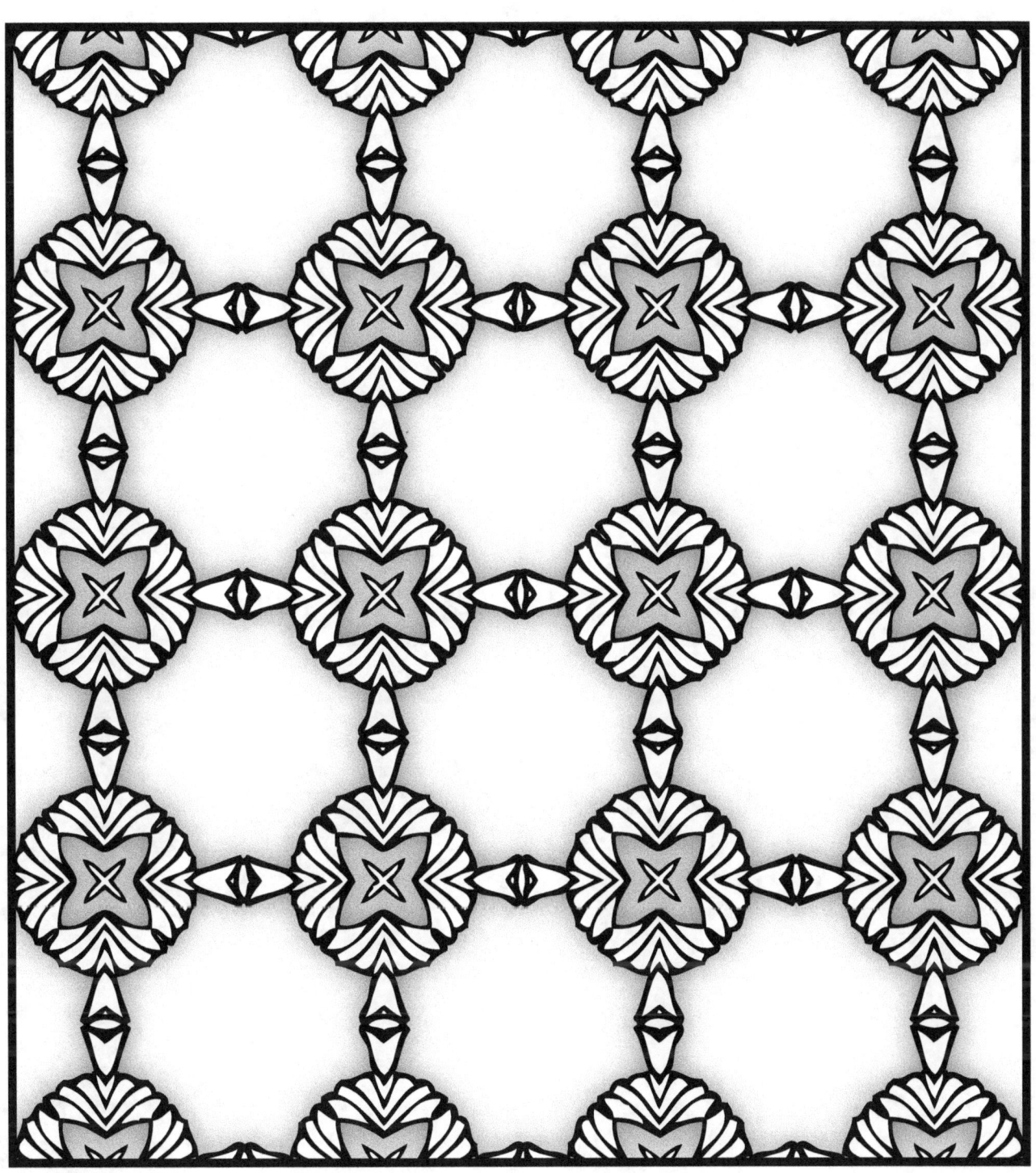

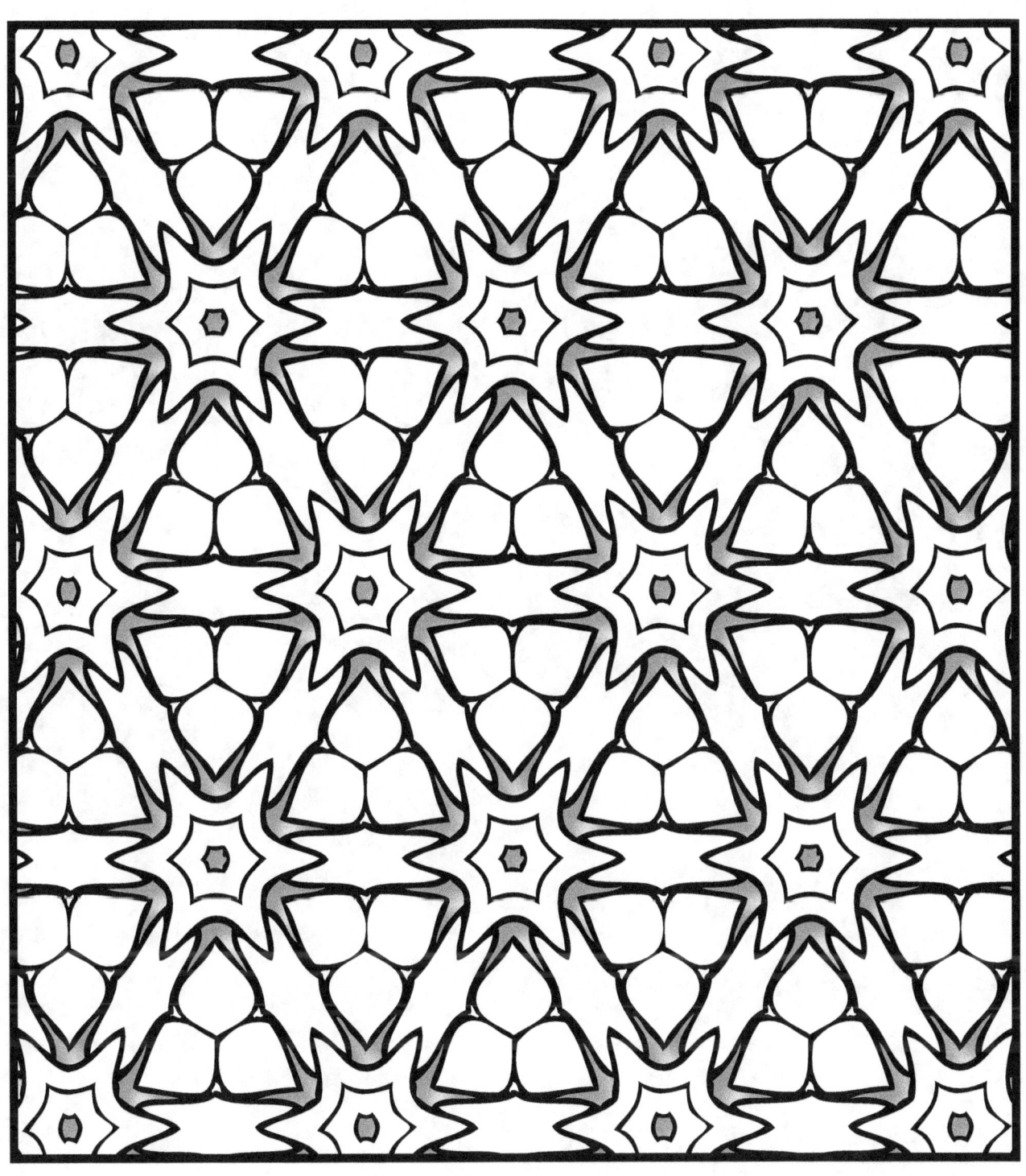

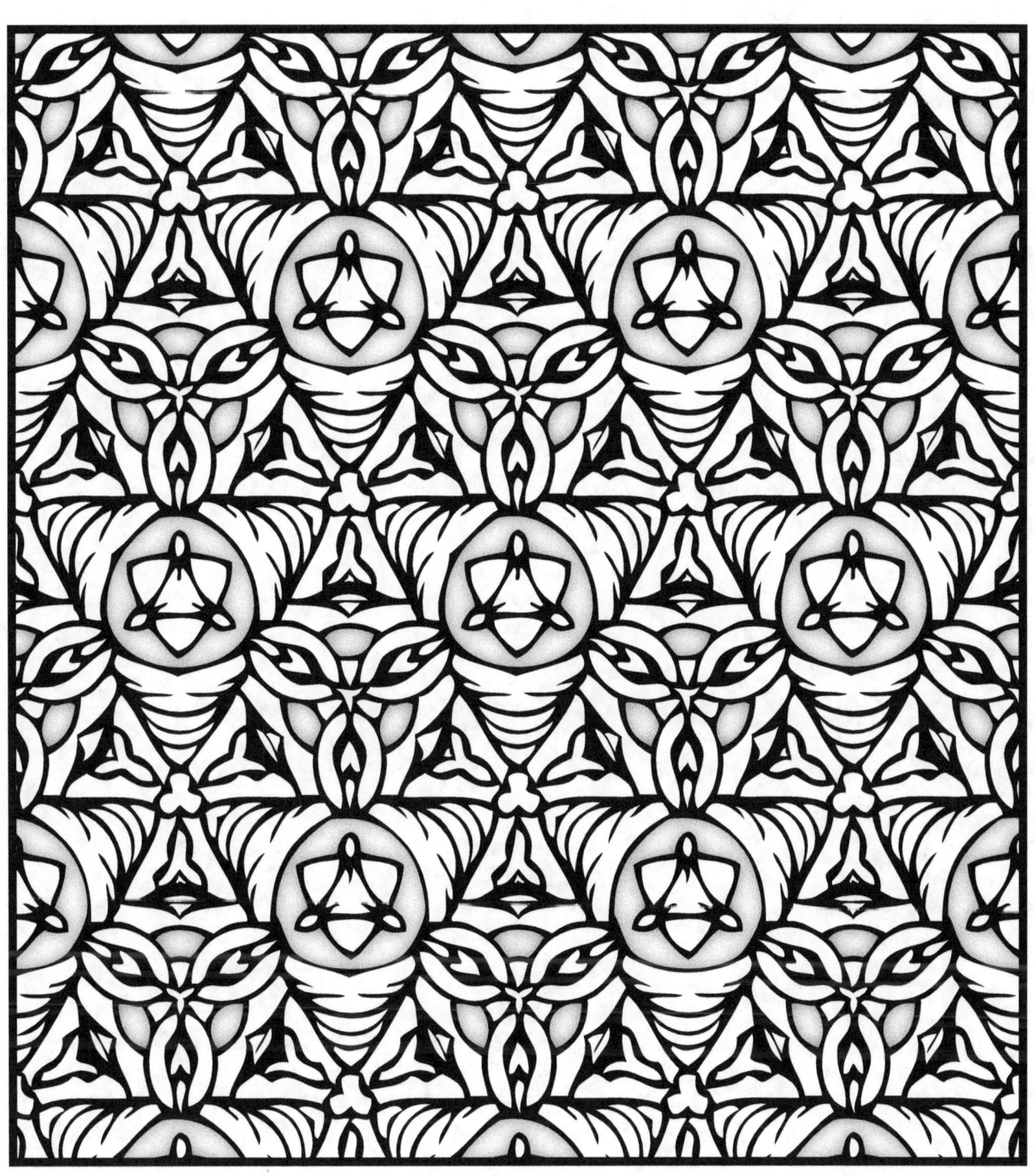

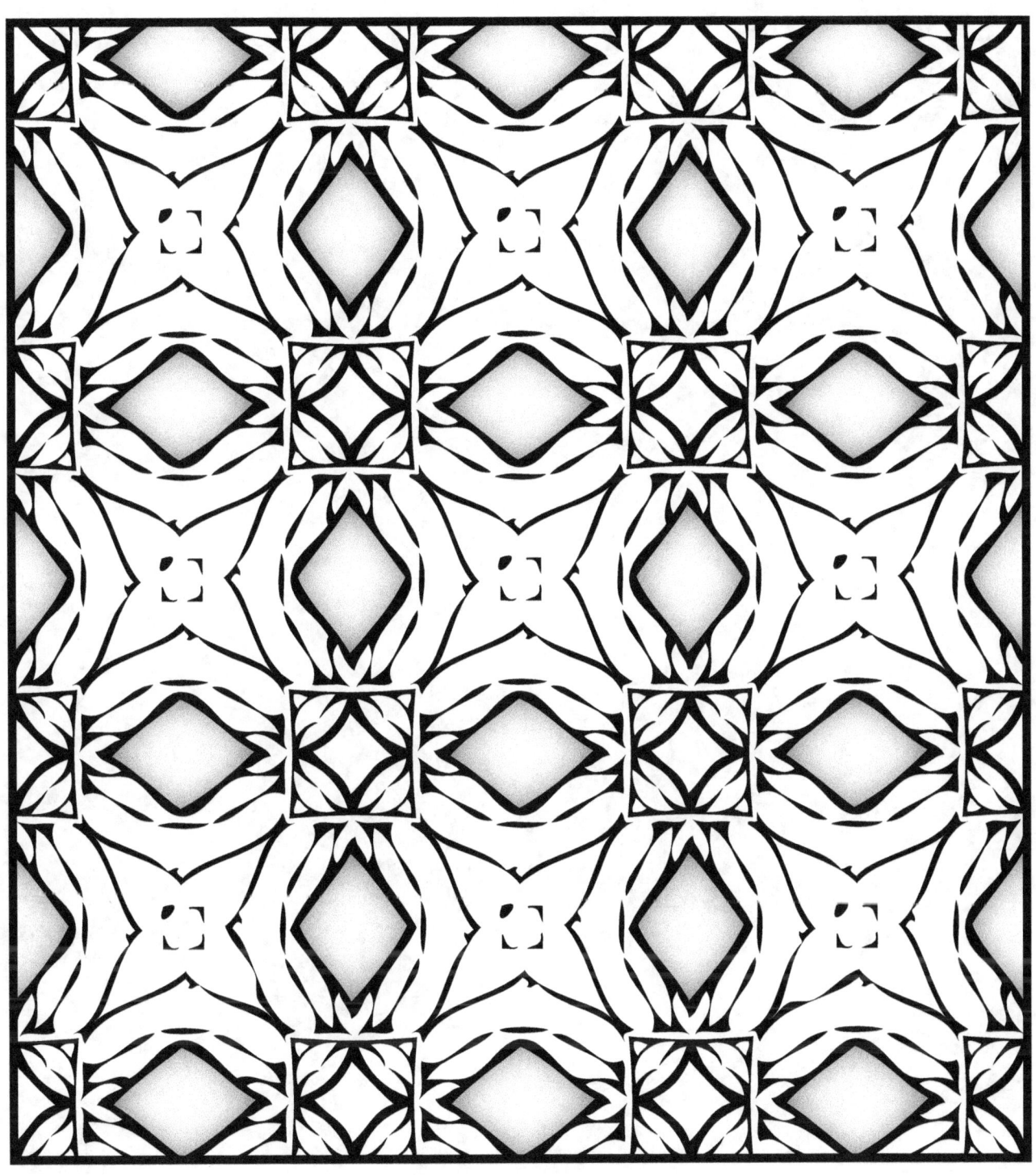

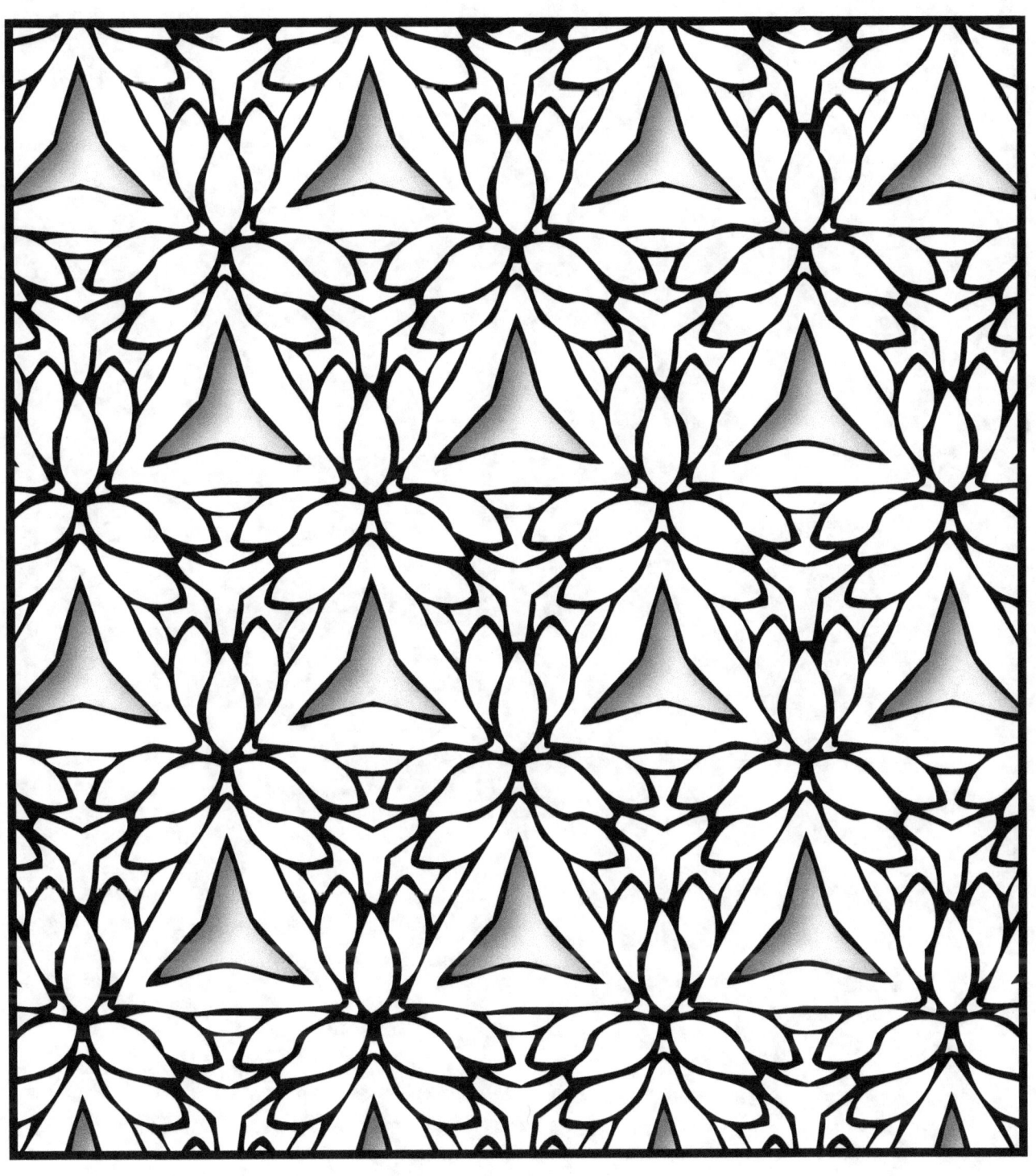

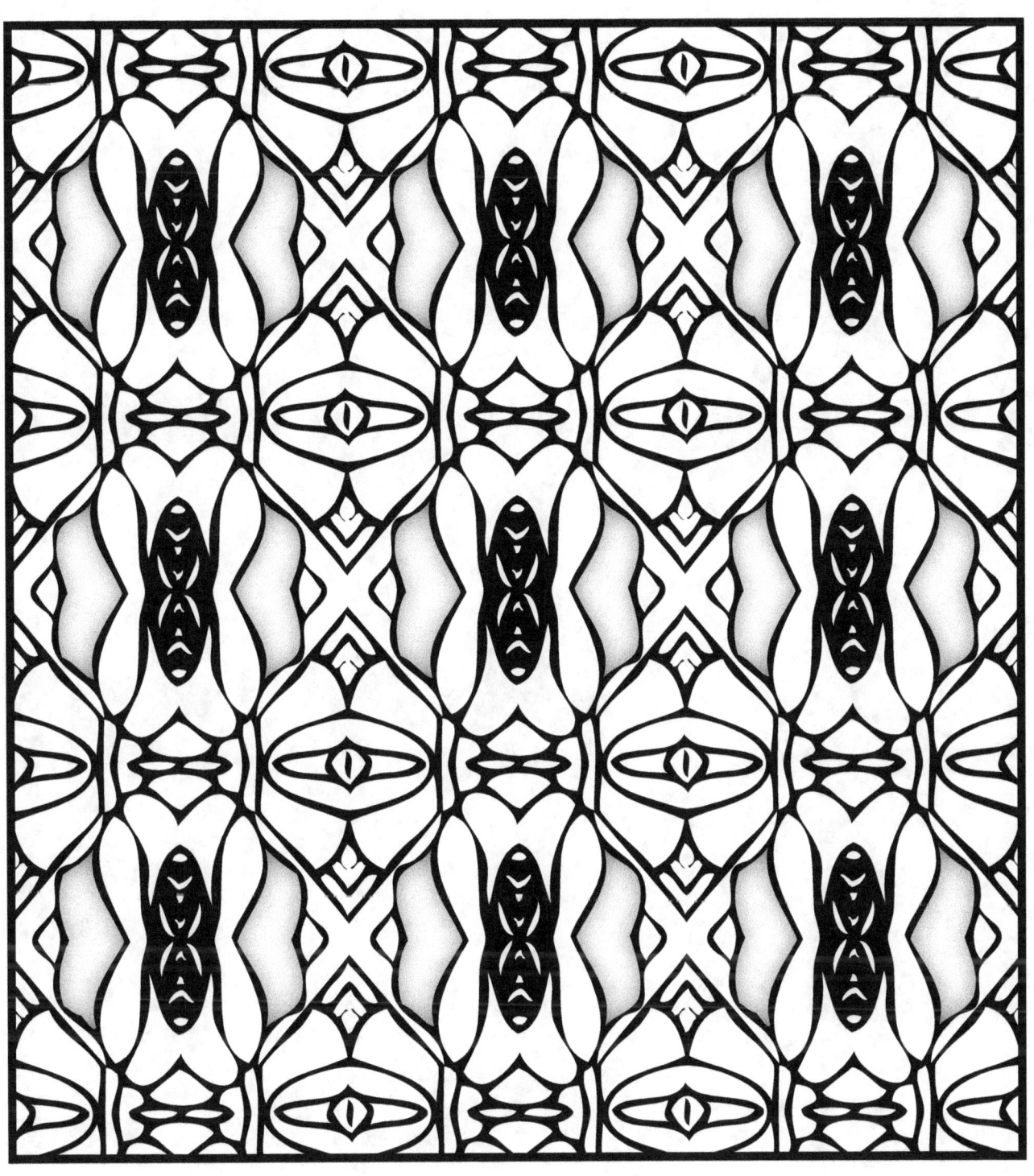

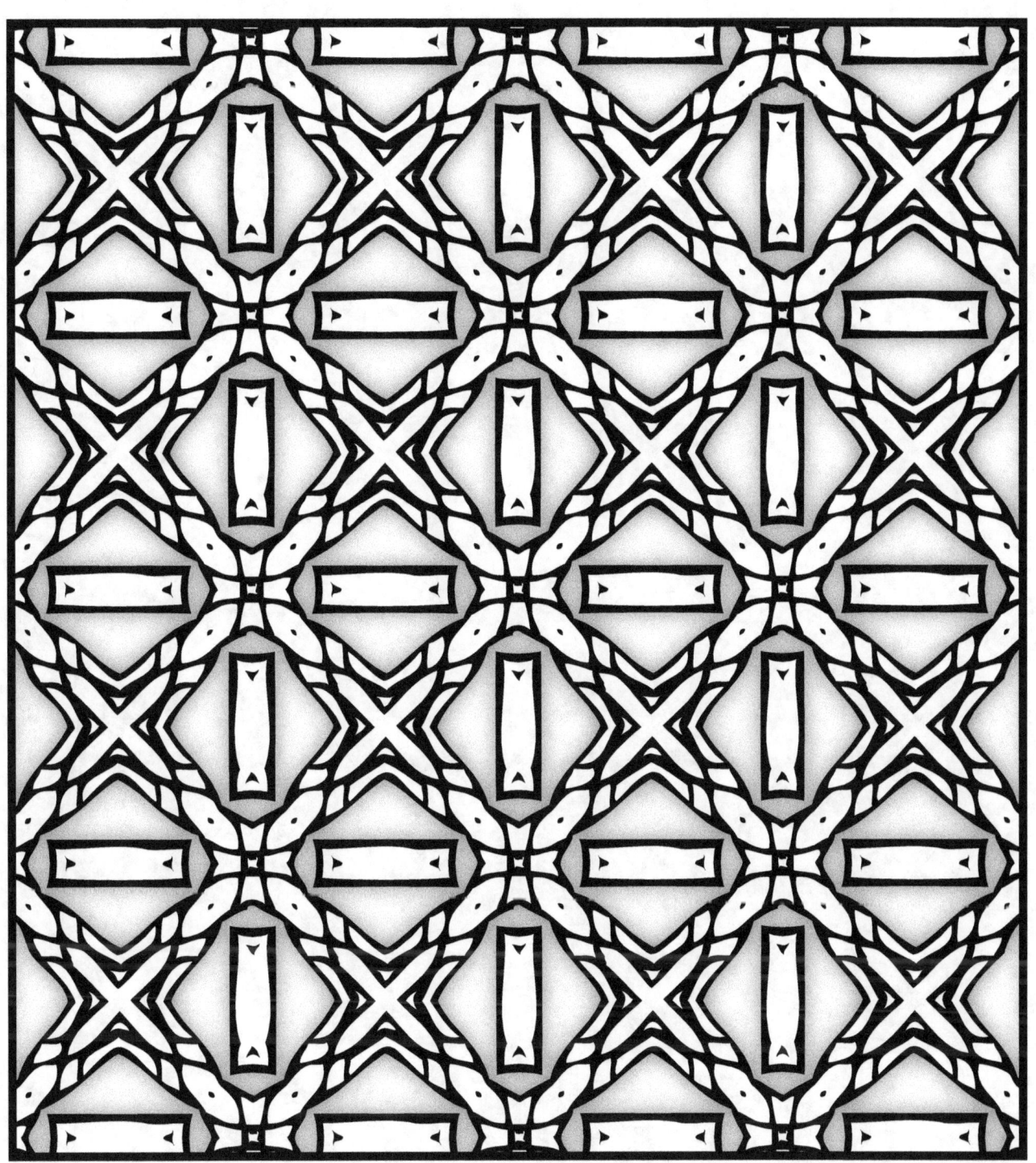

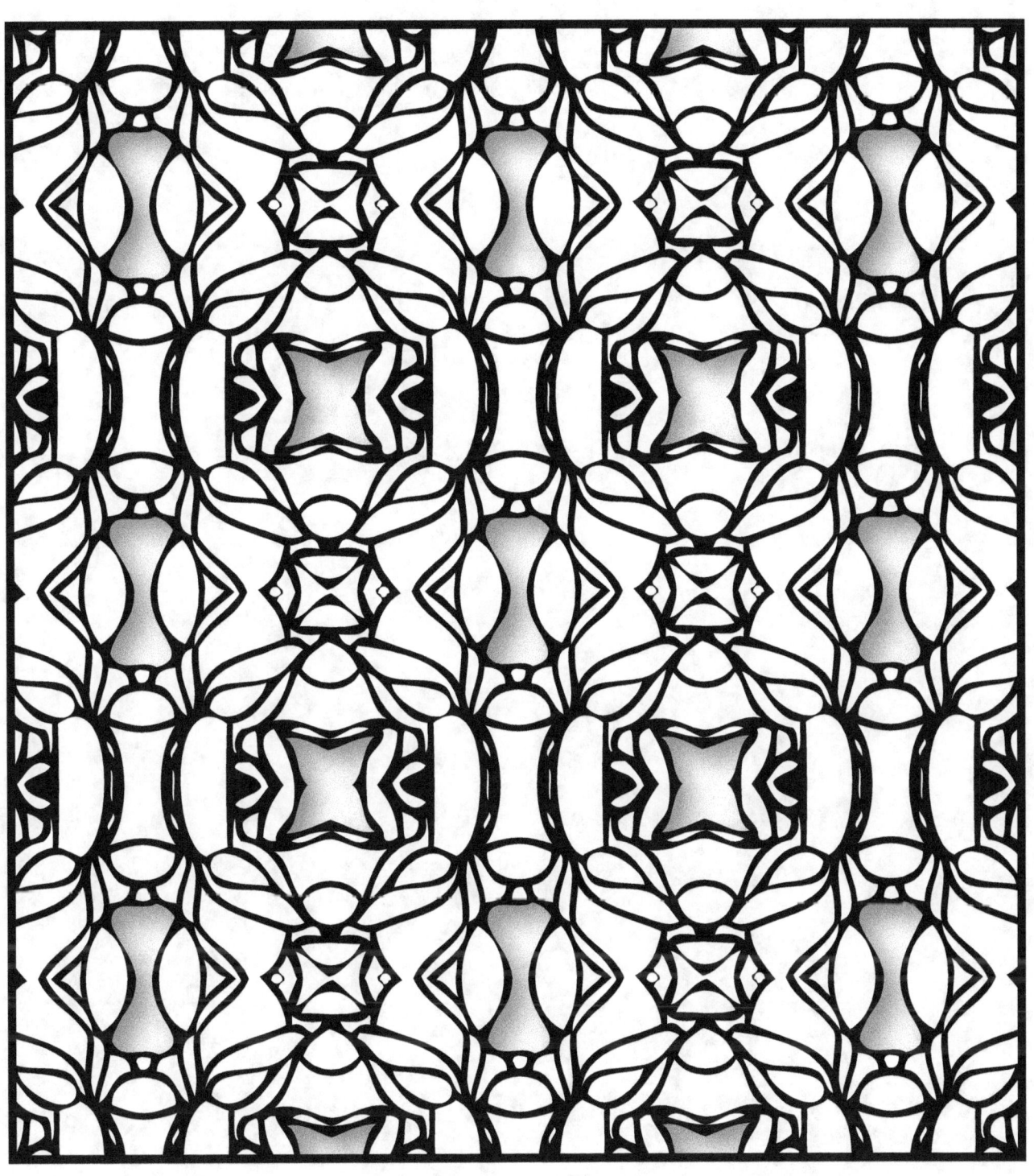

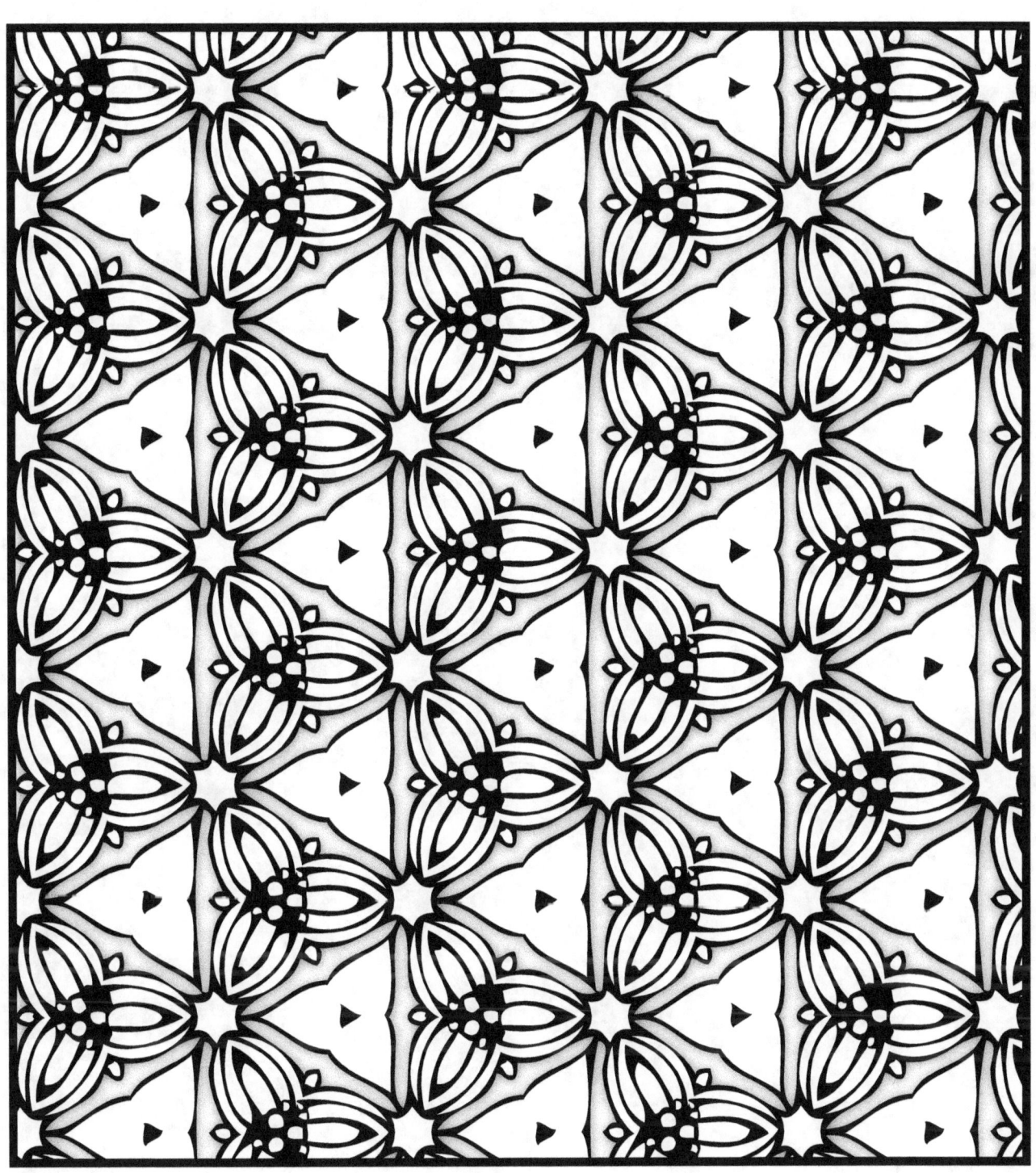

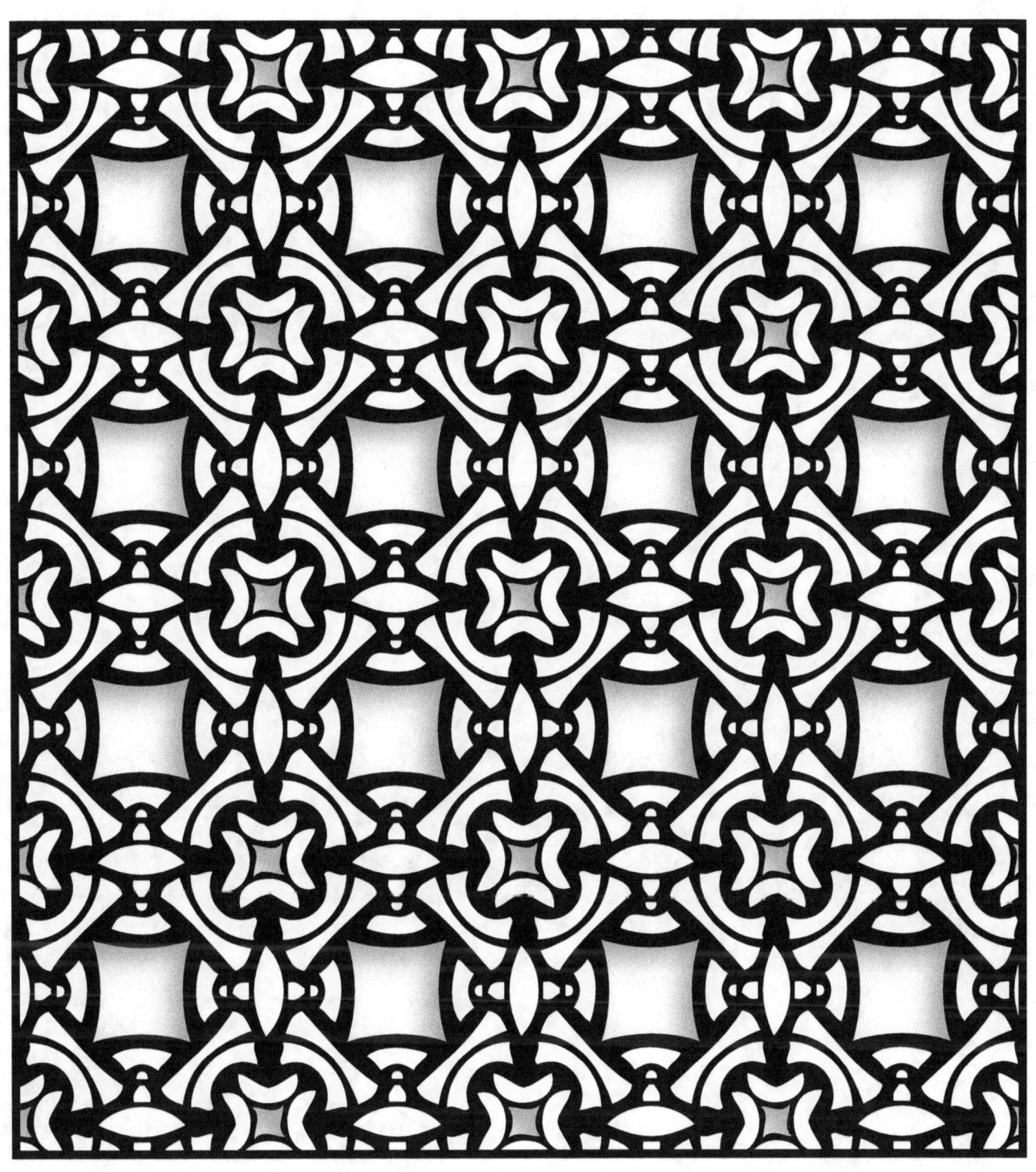

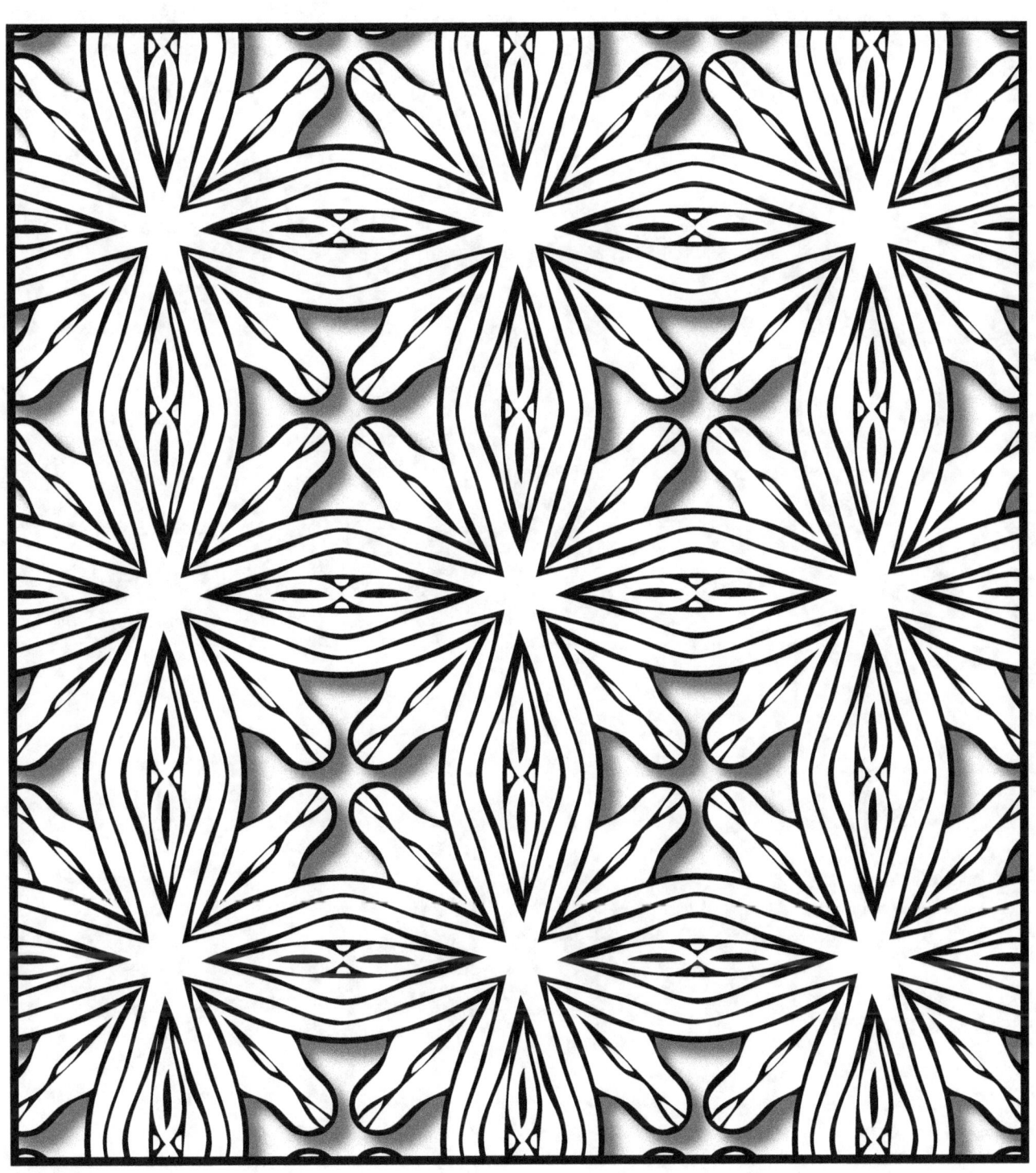

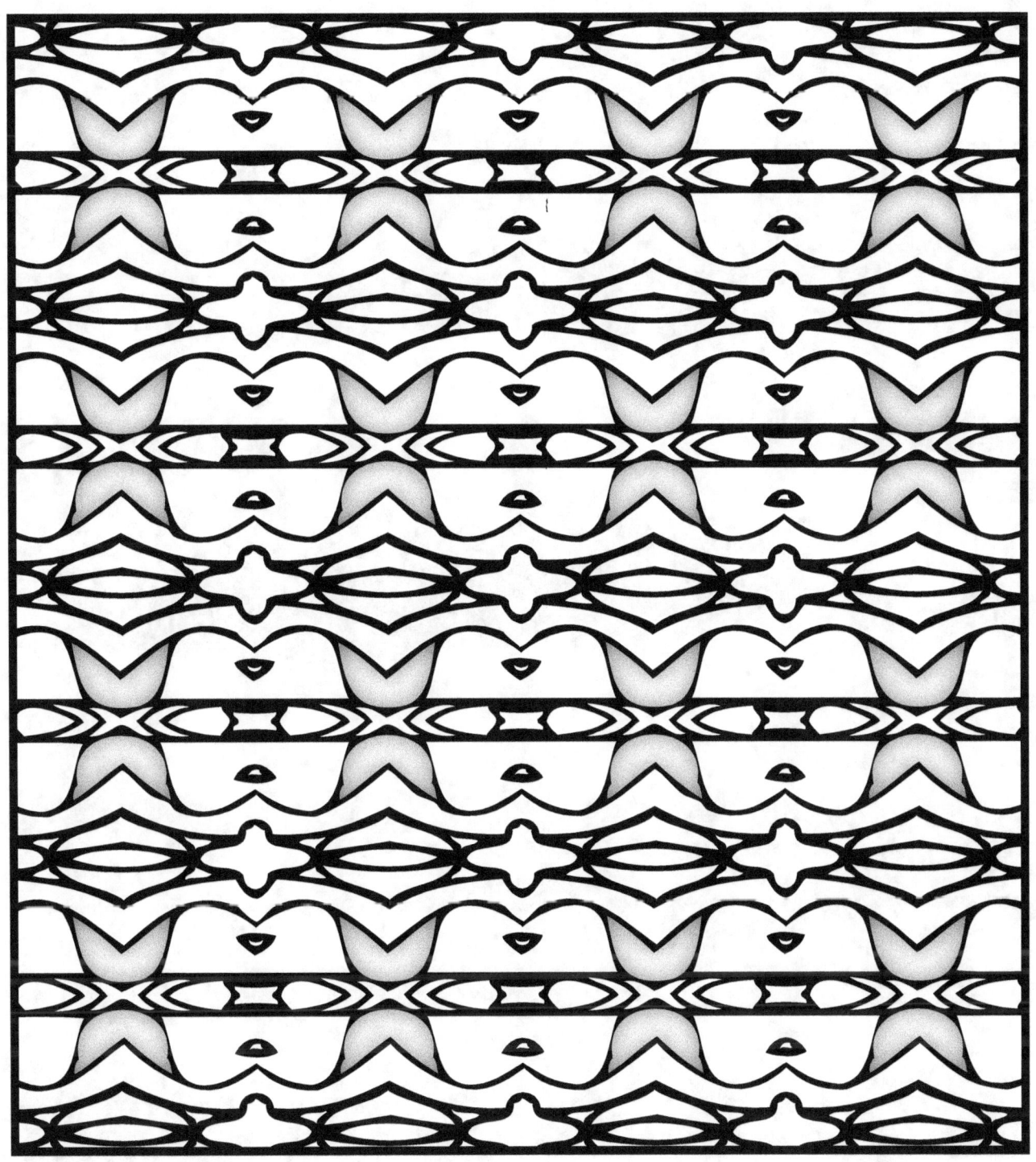

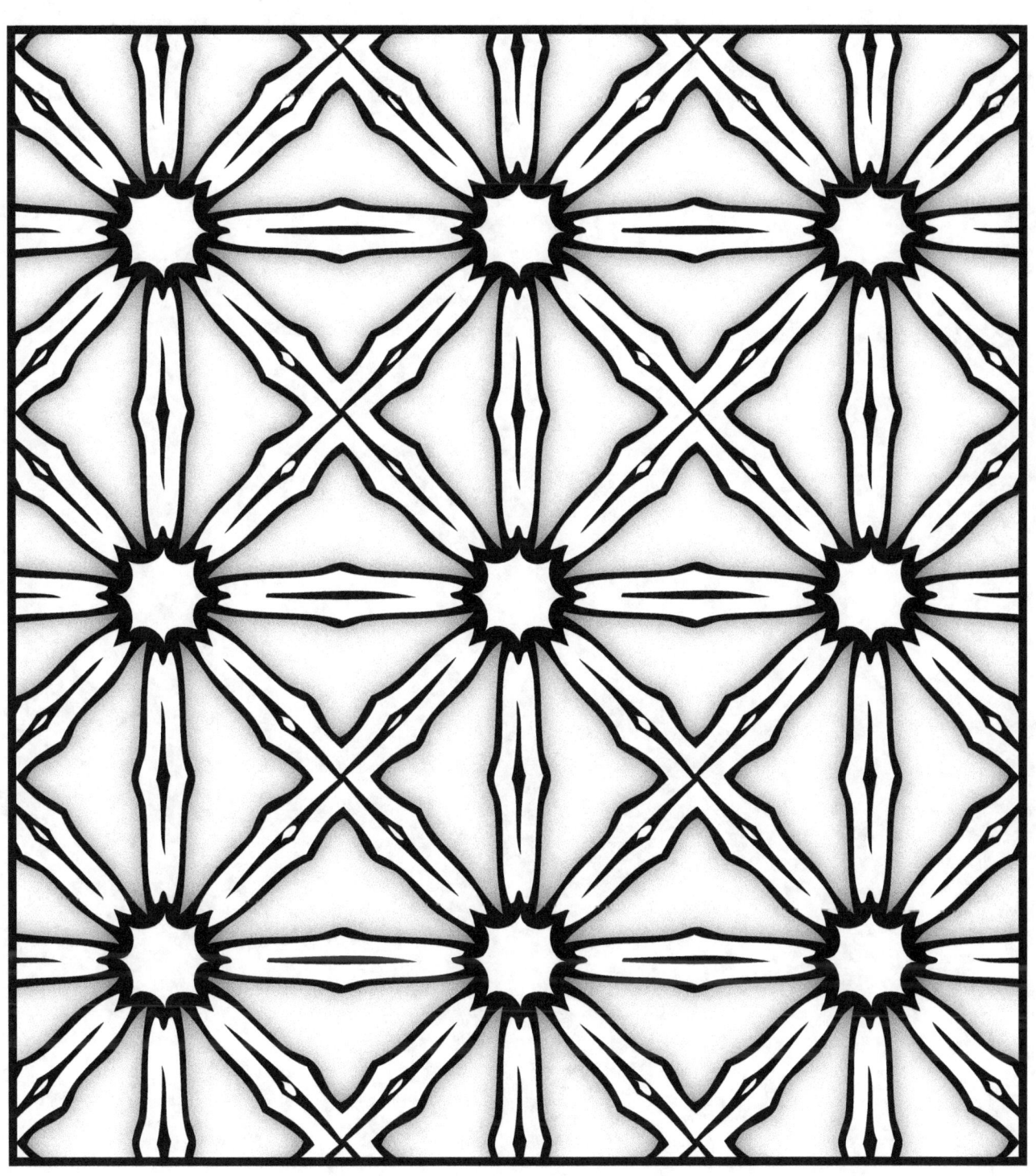

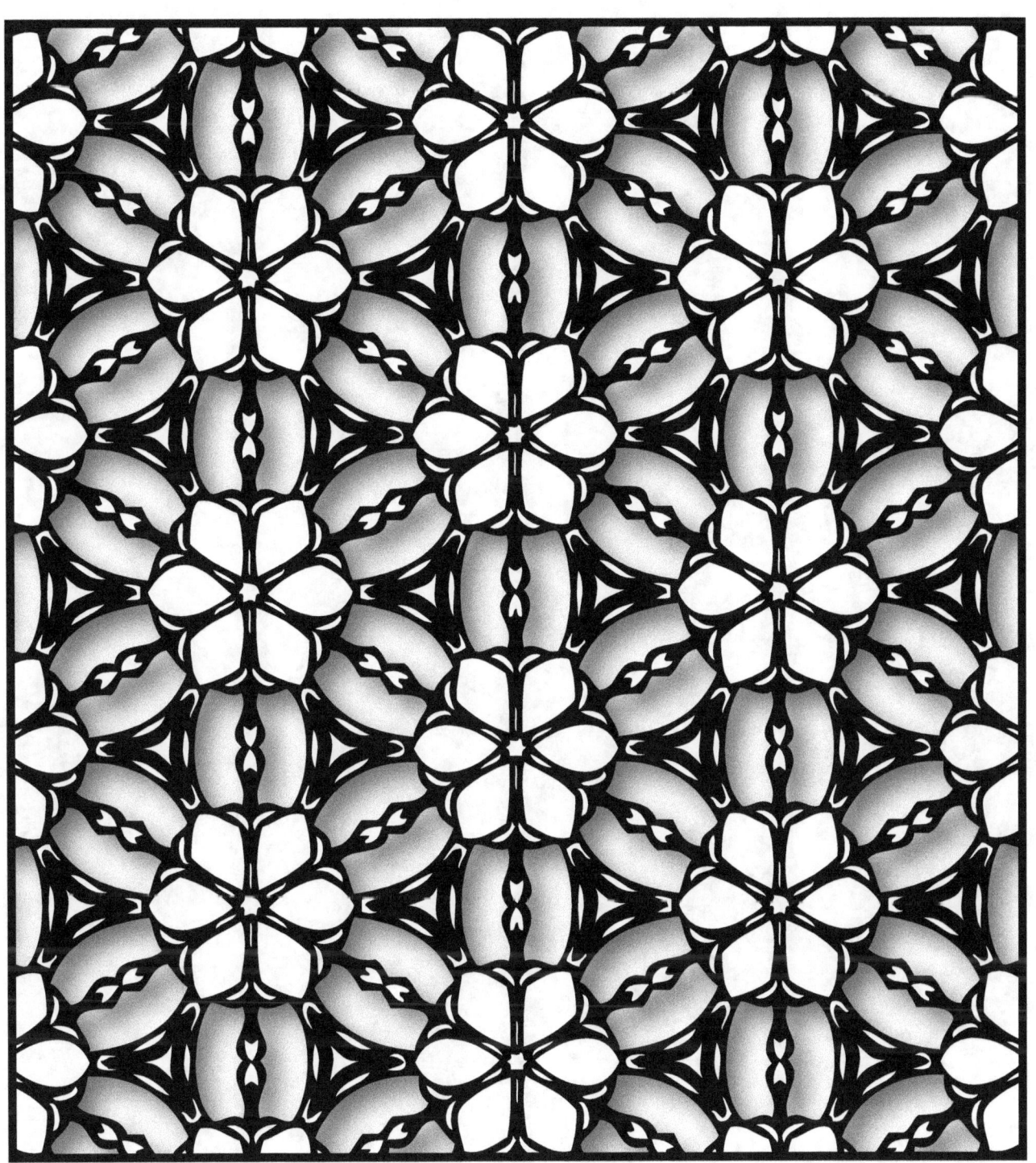

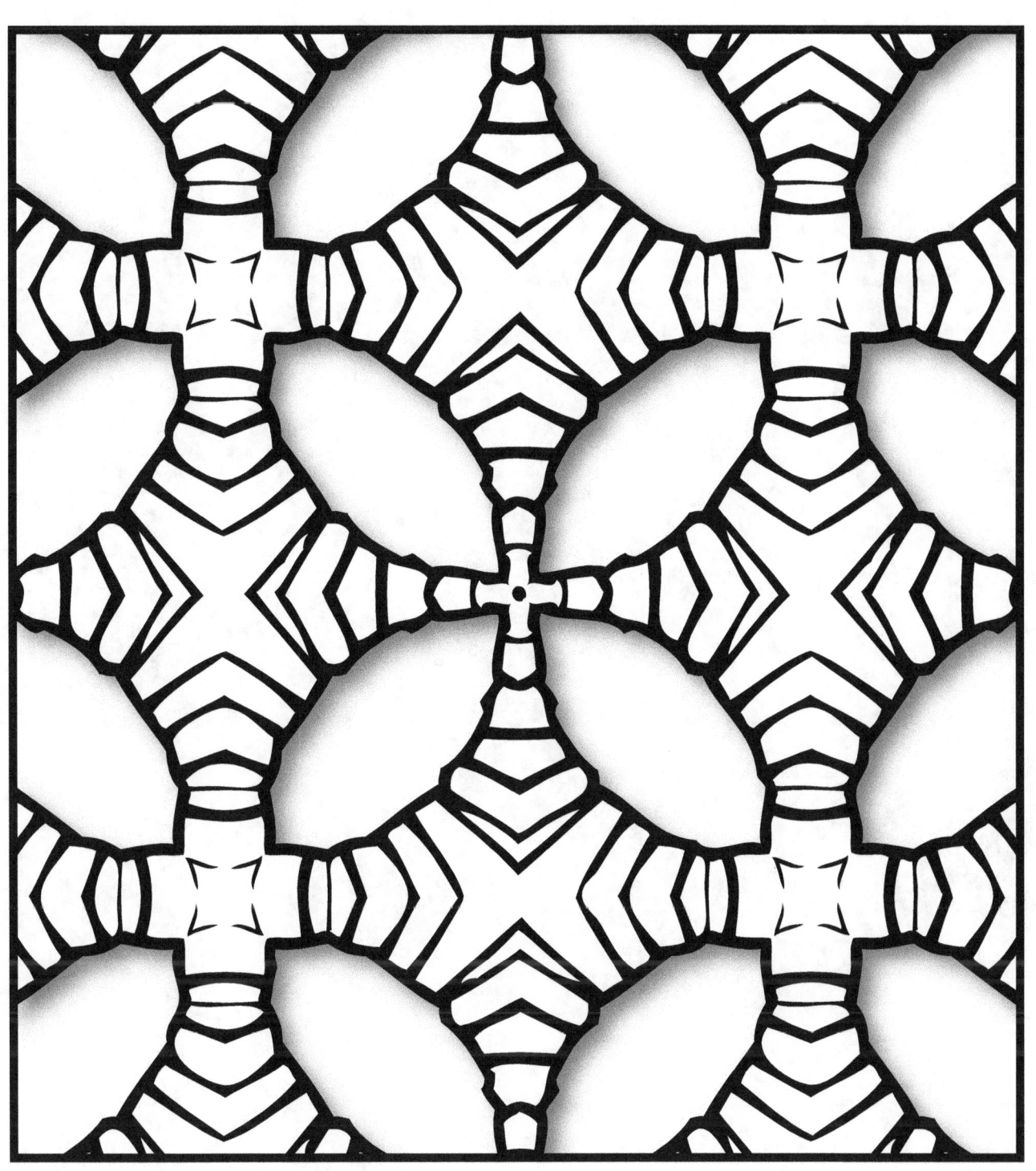

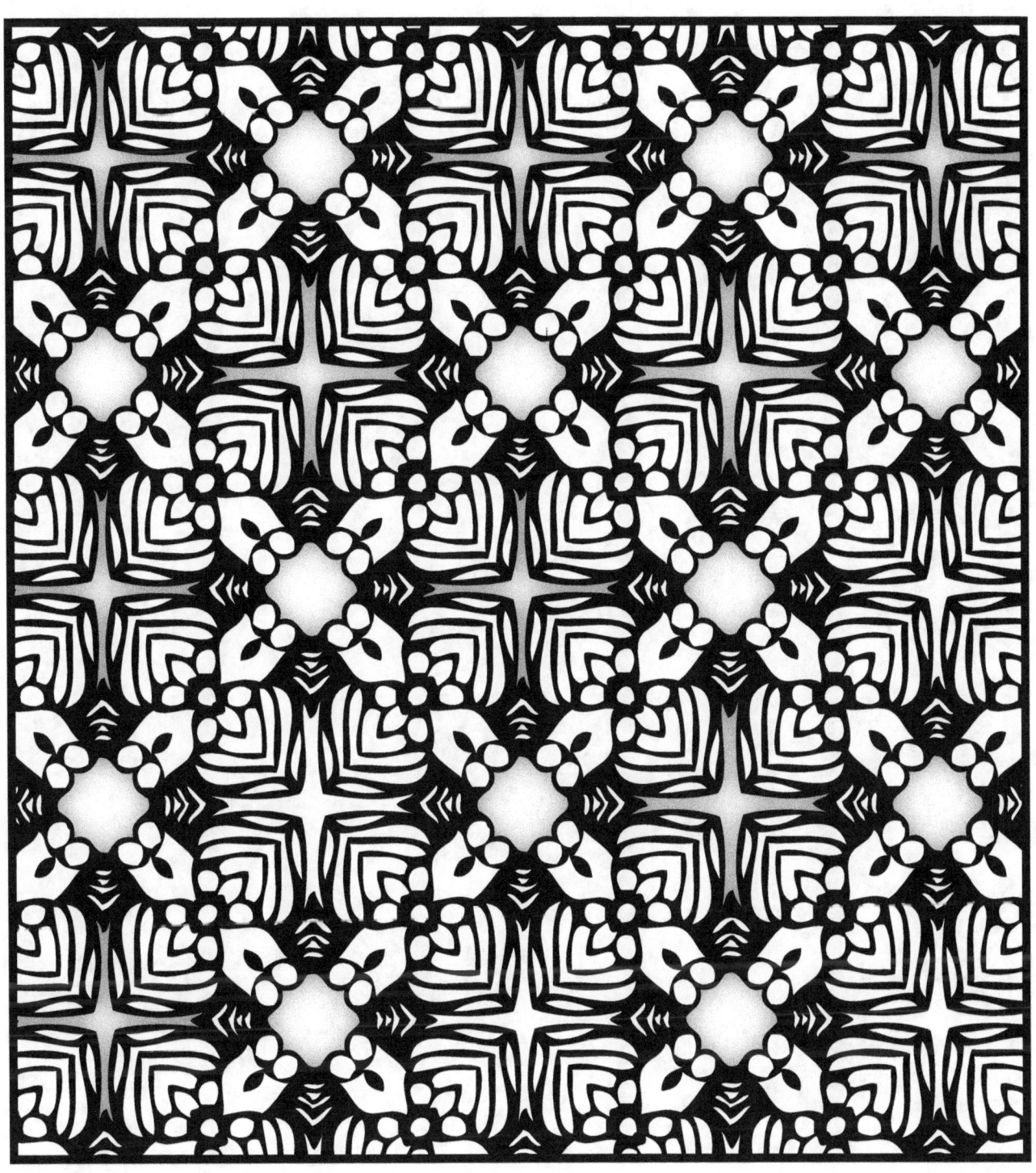

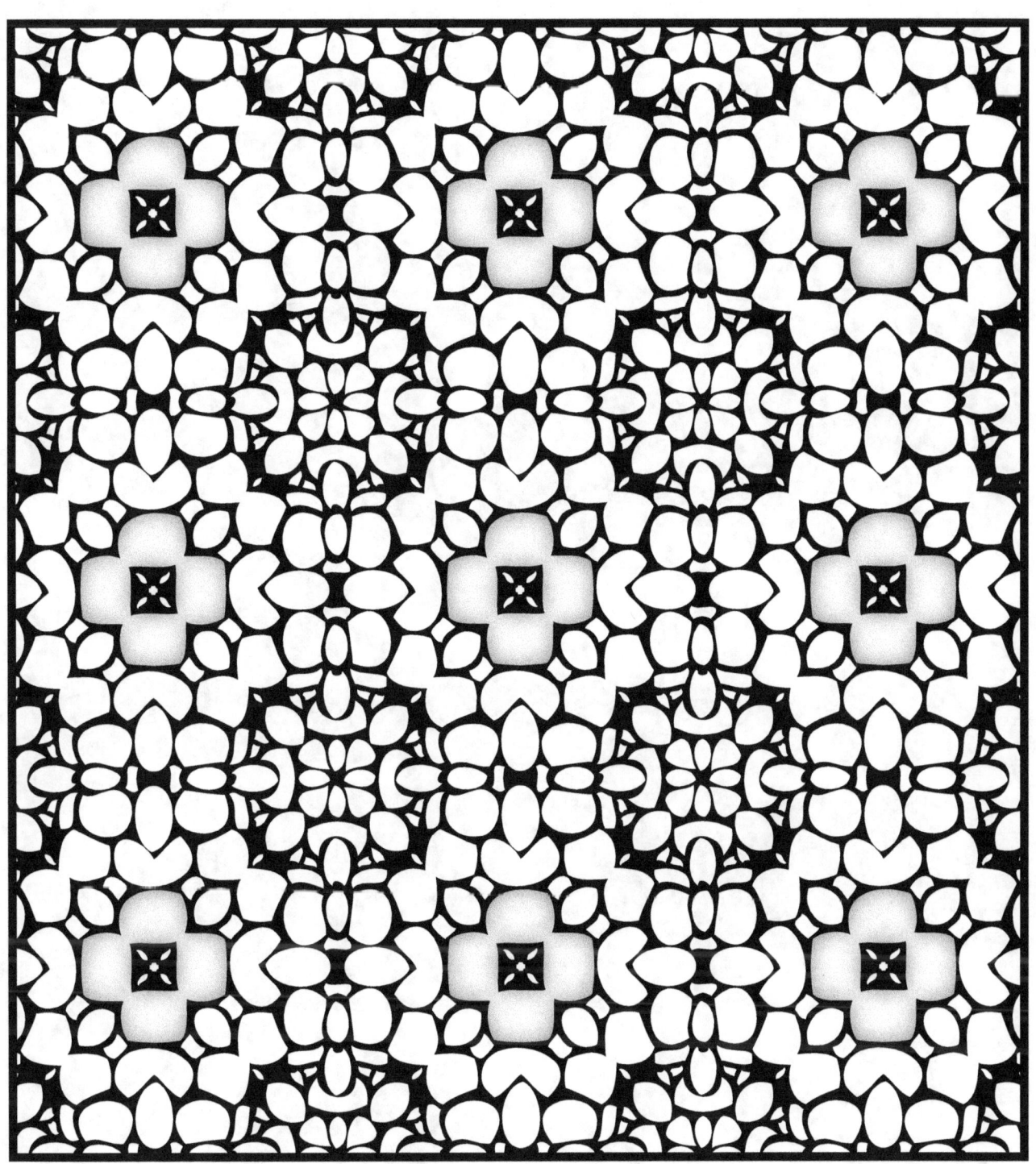

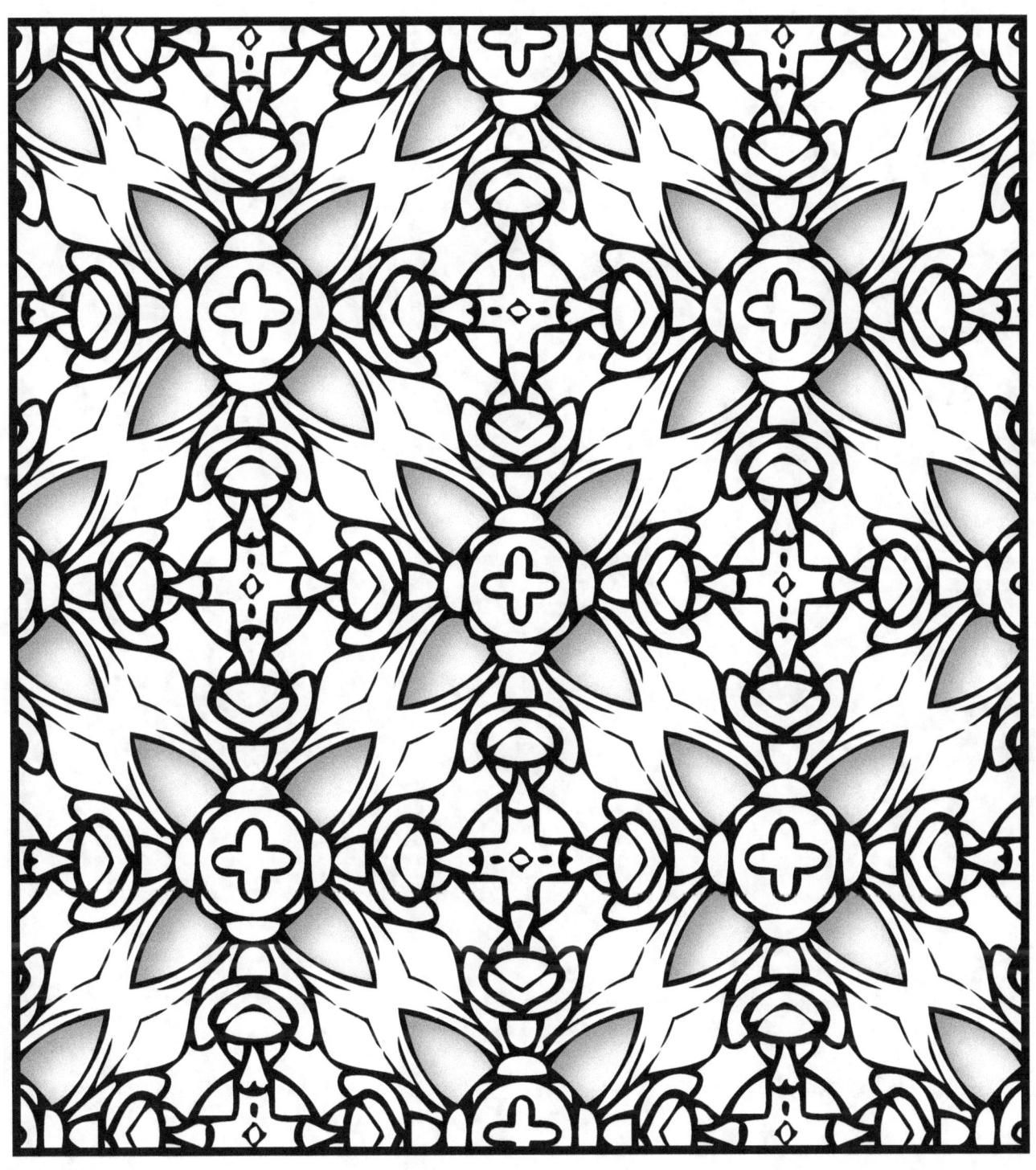

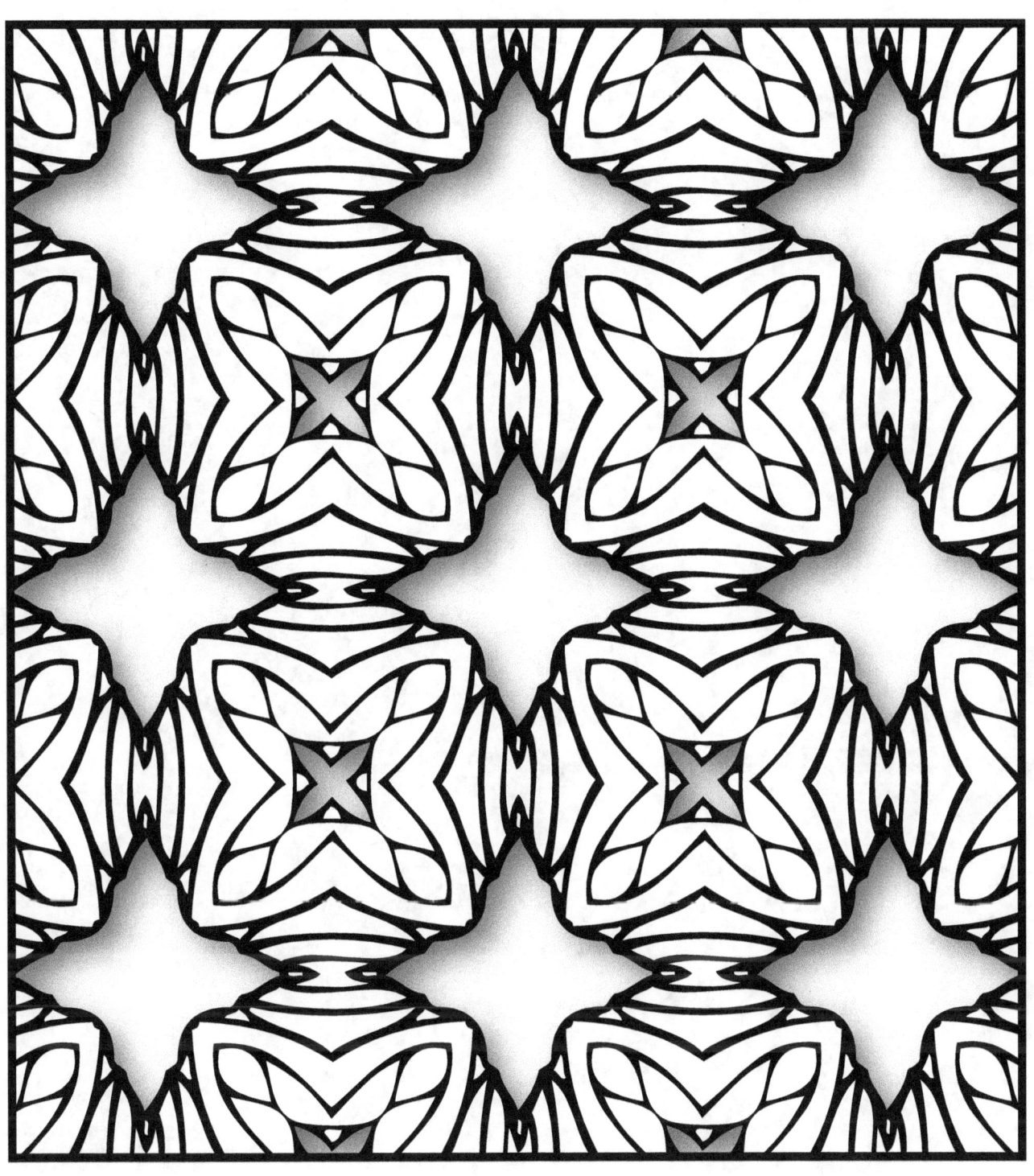

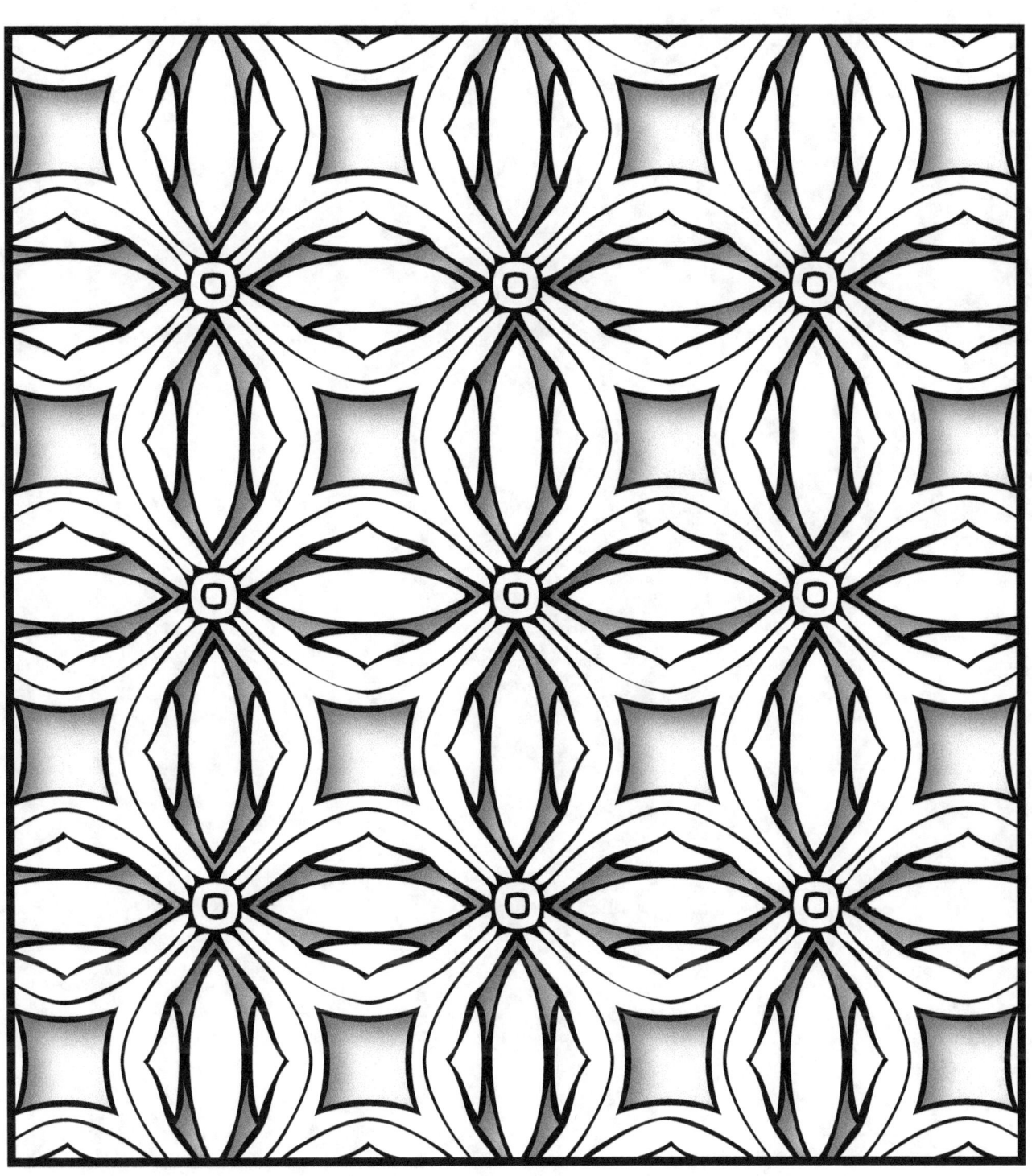

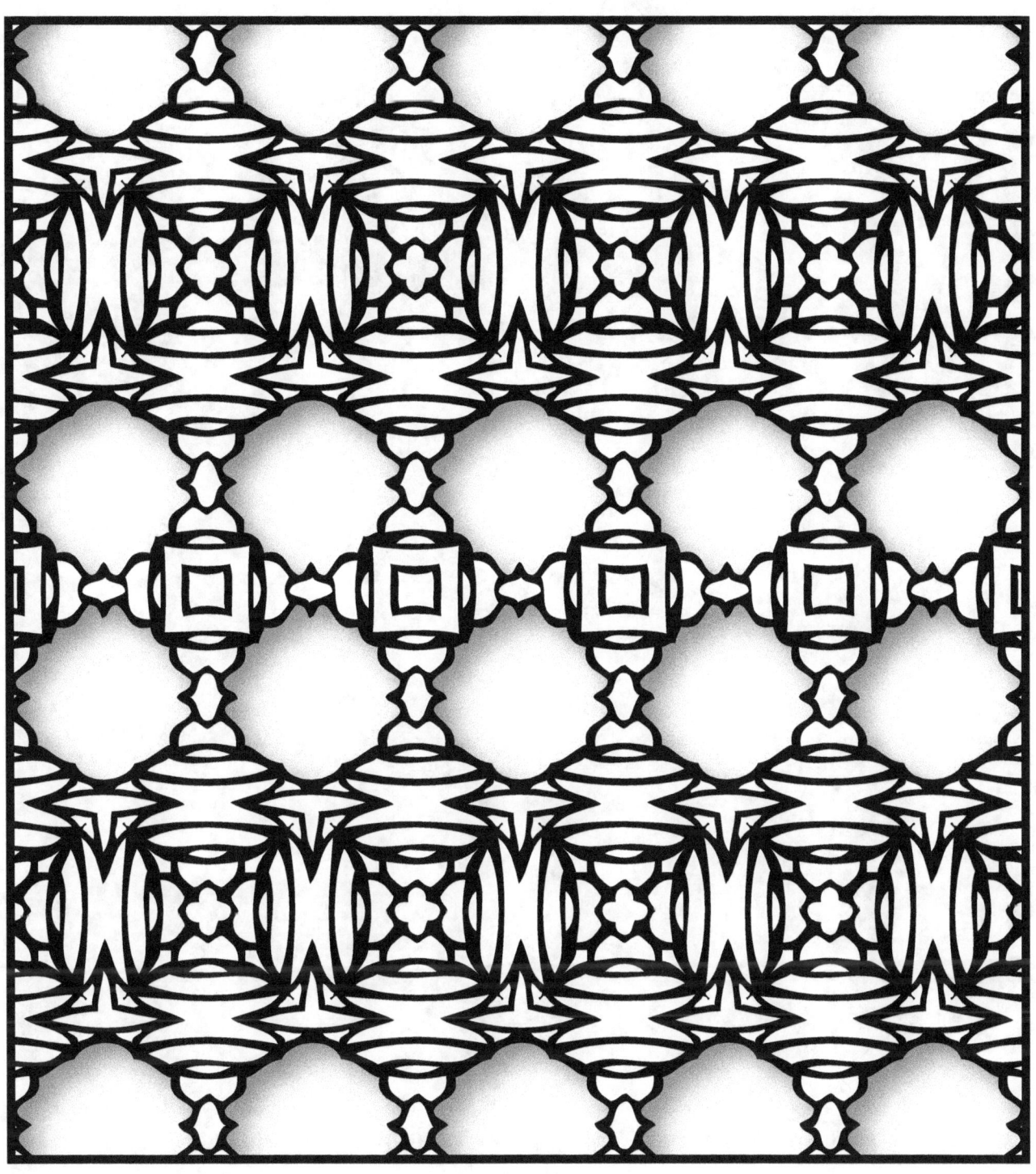

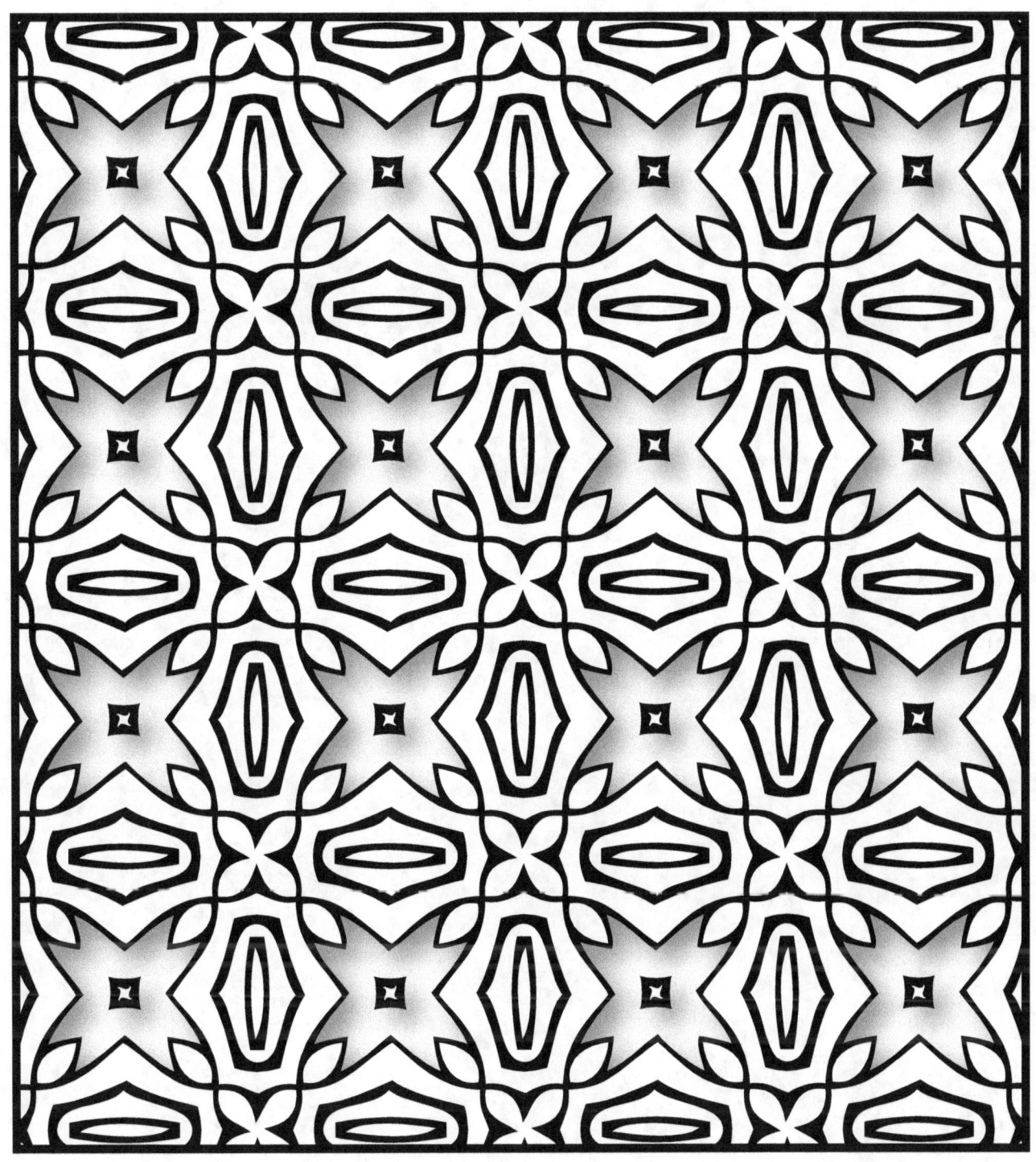

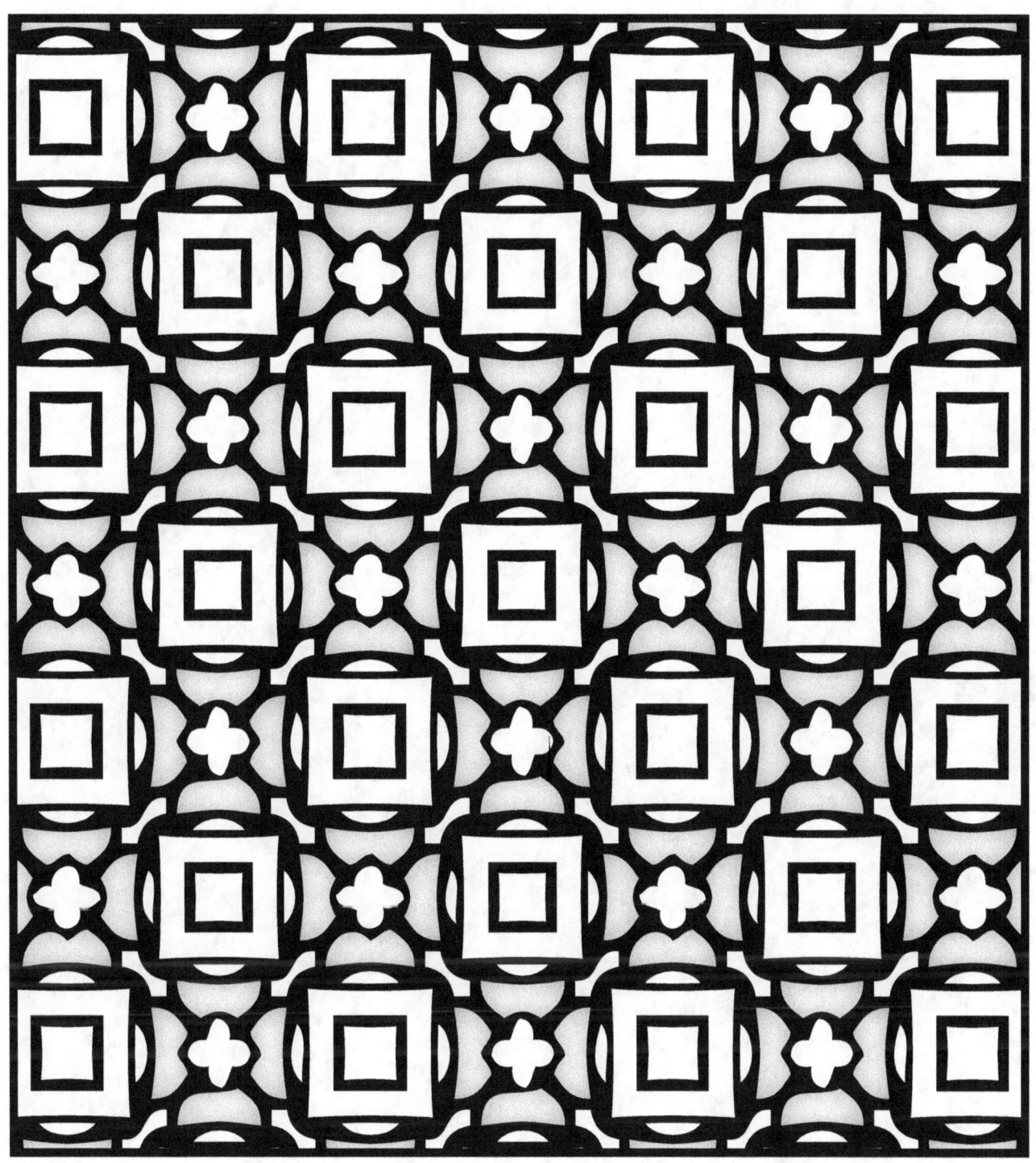

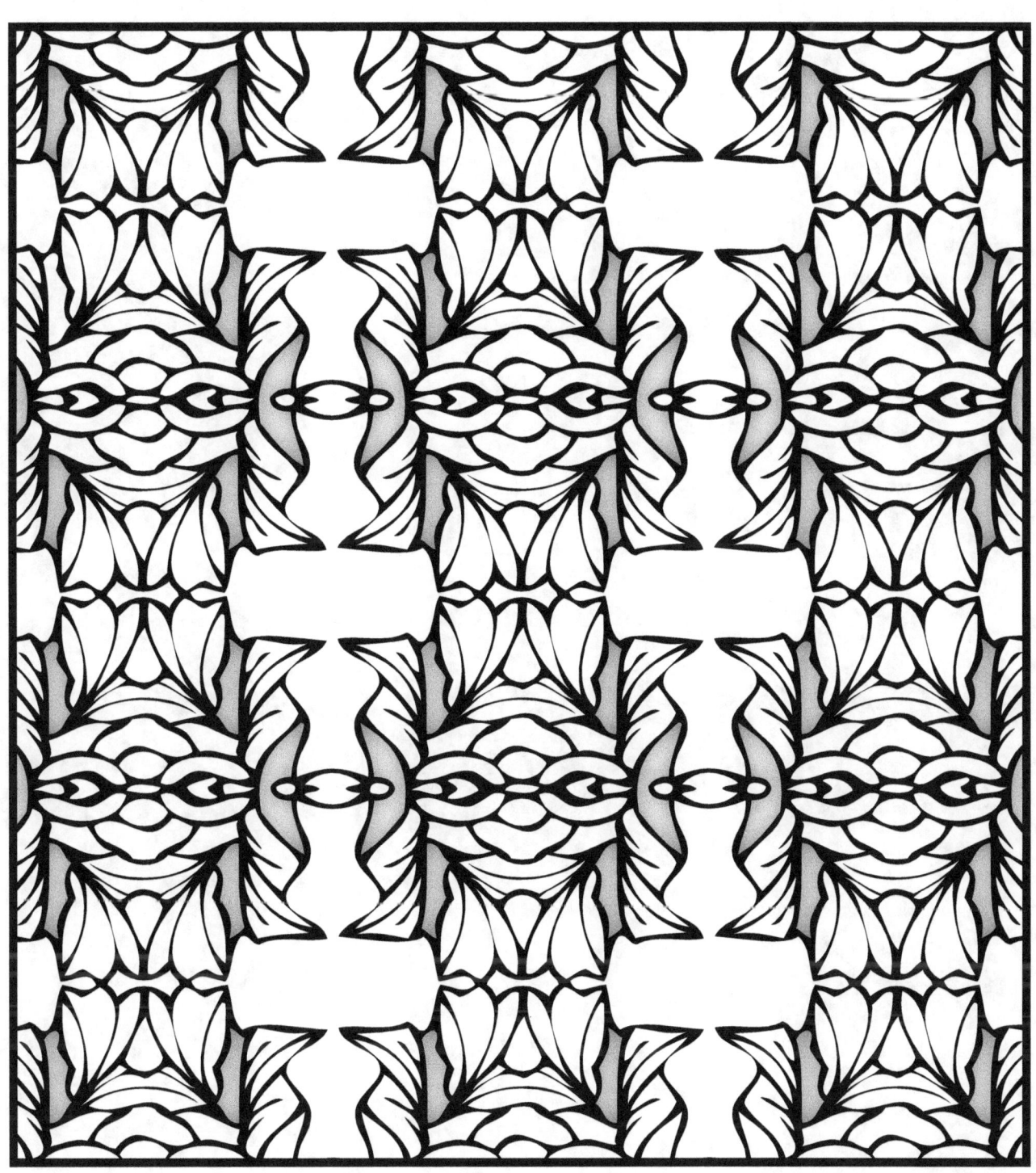

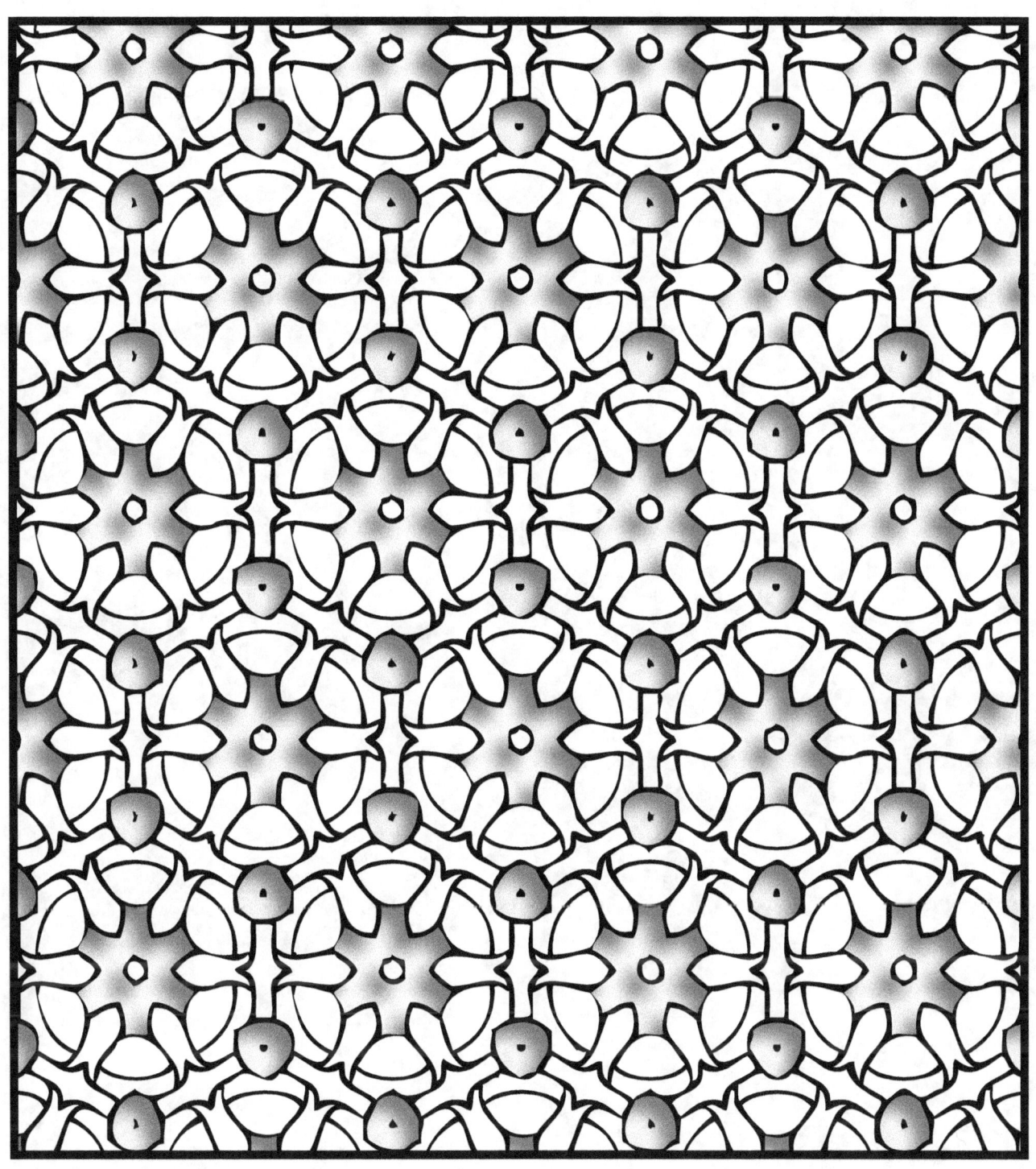

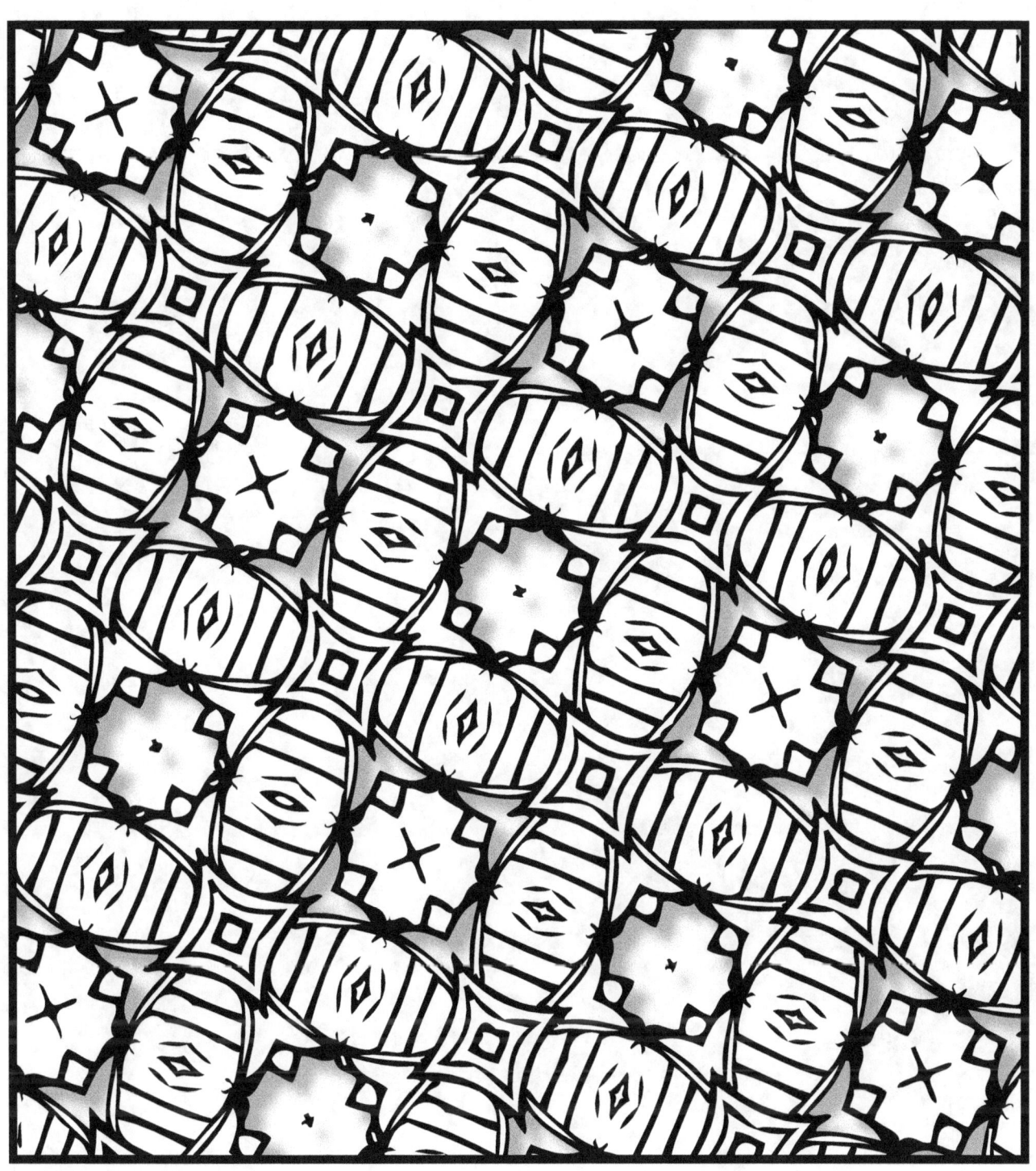

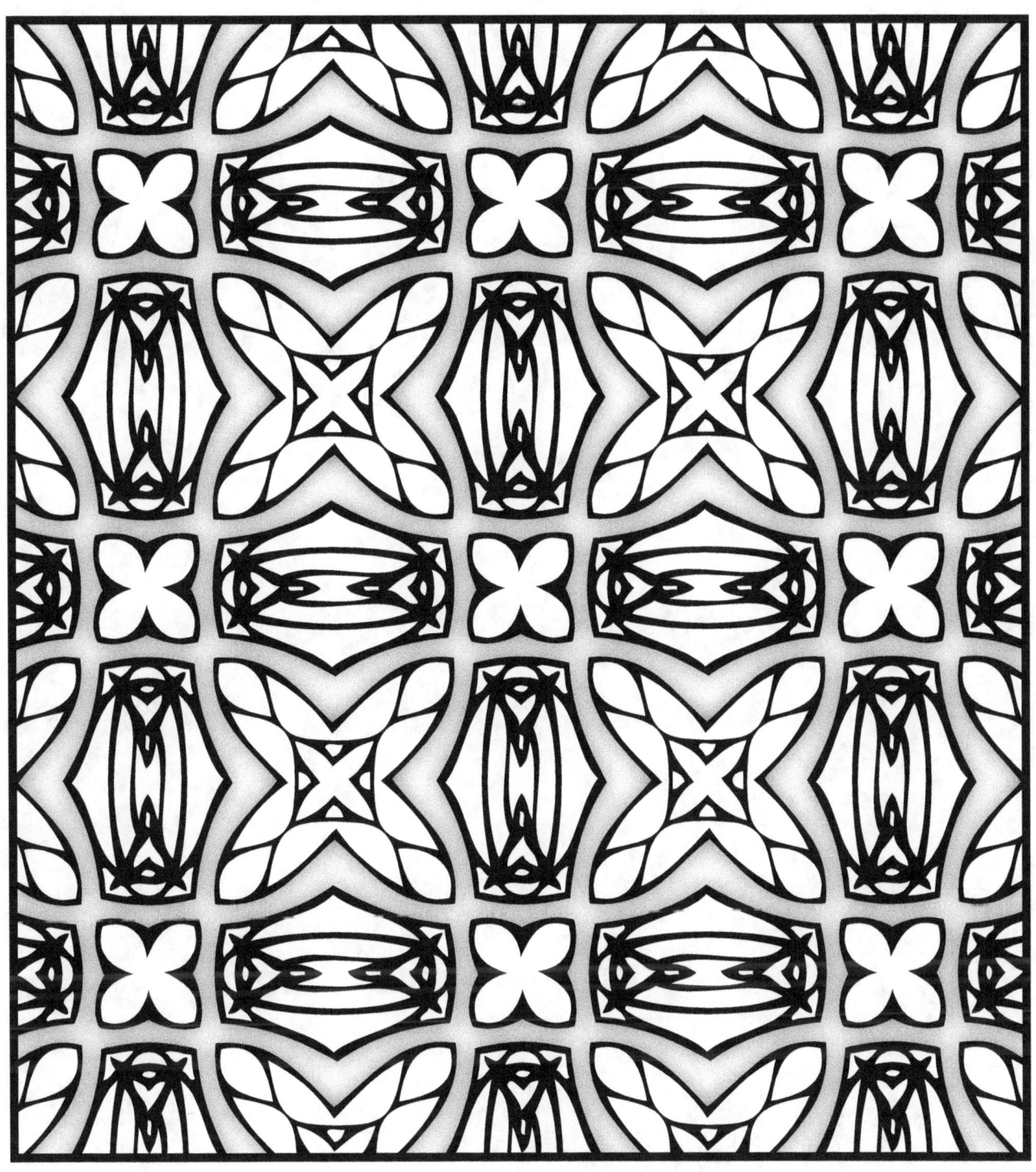

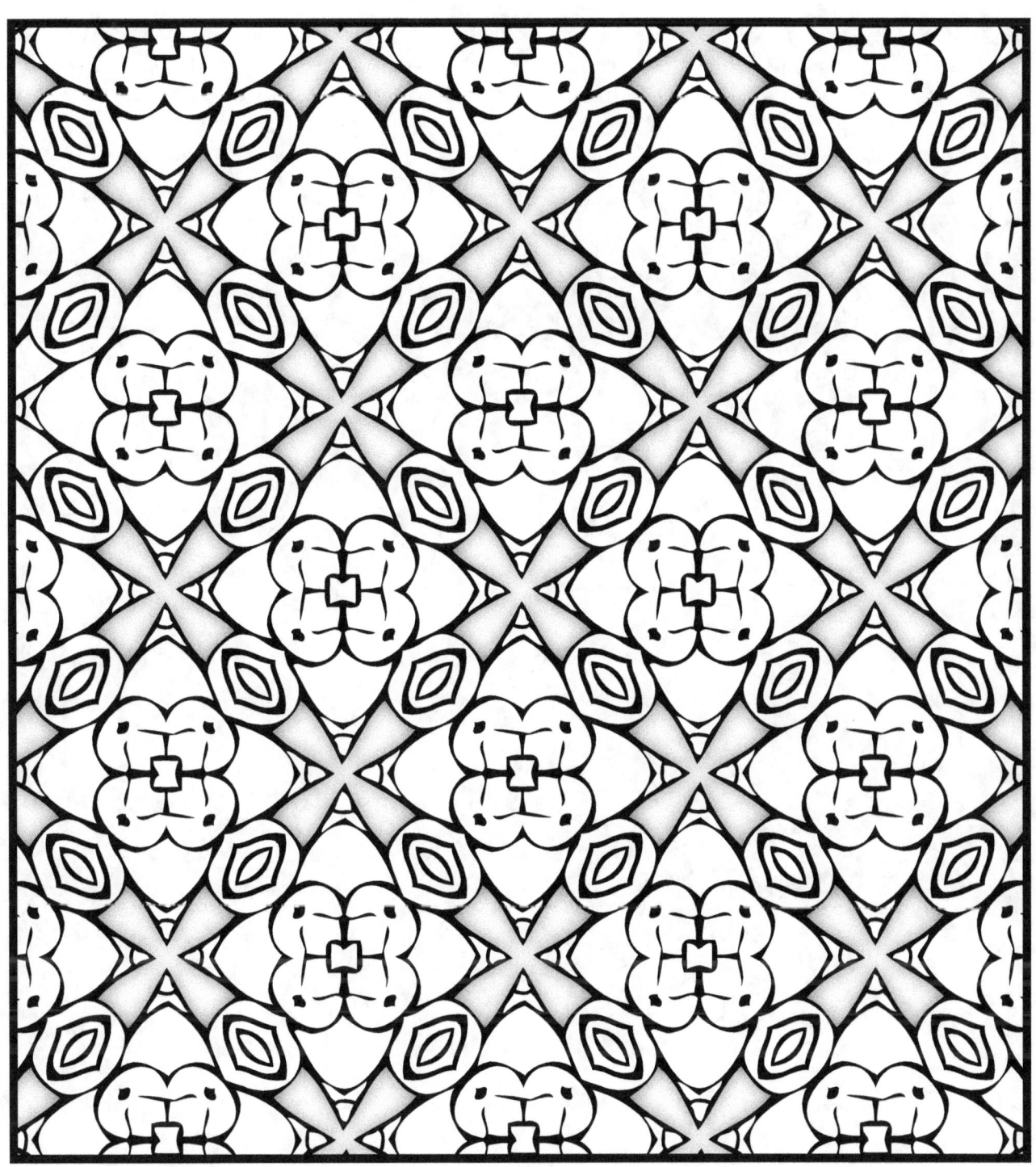

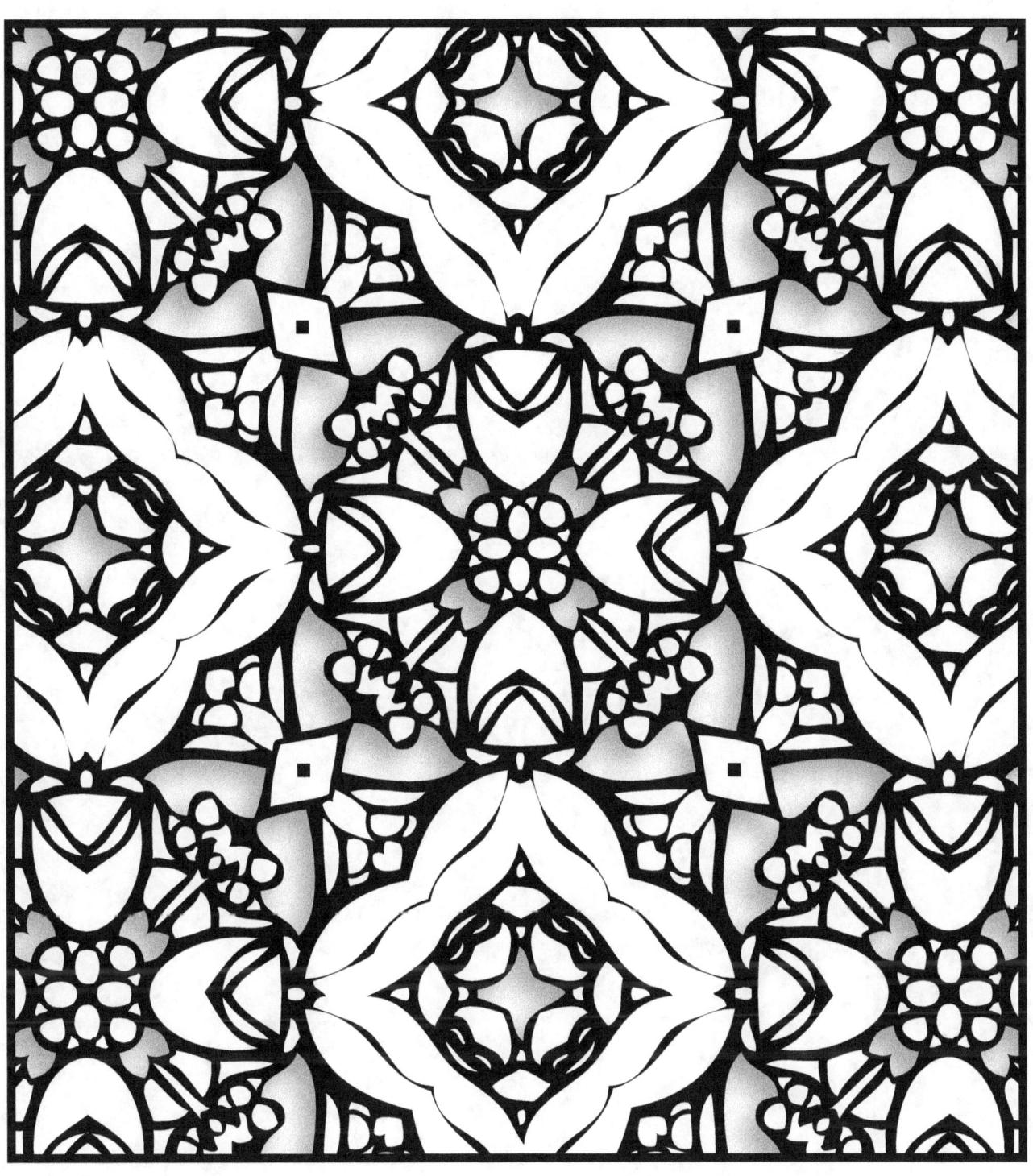

COLOR SWATCH TEST PAGE

Use this page to test and reference your colors

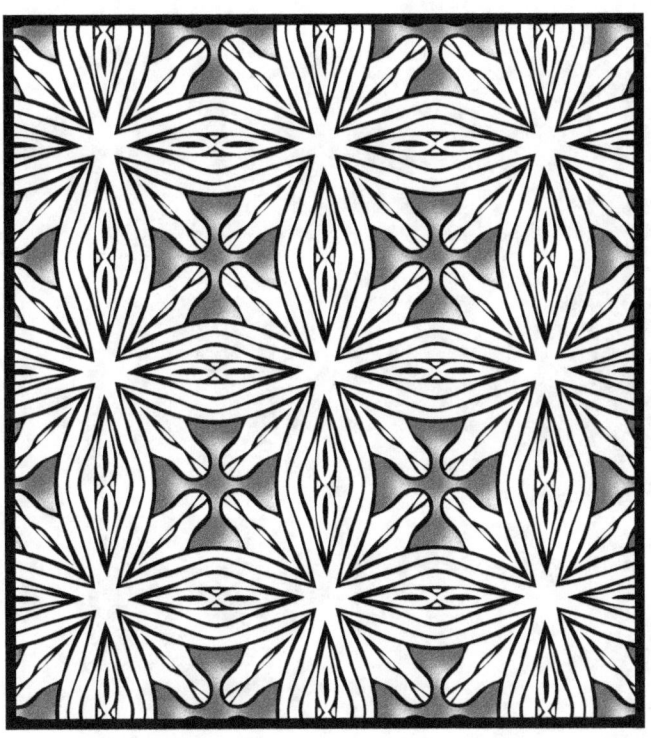

Shadowboxes 2 Coloring Book
© 2016 Paula Parrish

www.lovelyleisure.me